MORE
PUB W
IN HAMPSHIRE

Thirty Circular Walks

Around Hampshire Inns

Mike Power
John Quarendon

Other publications in the series
Pub Walks in Dorset
40 More Pub Walks in Dorset
Pub Walks in Hampshire
Pub Walks in Devon
Pub Walks in Somerset
Pub Walks in East Sussex
Pub Walks in West Sussex
Pub Walks in Kent
Pub Walks in North Surrey
Pub Walks in South Surrey
40 More Pub Walks in Surrey
Pub Walks in the New Forest
Pub Walks in Hardy's Wessex
Dorset Tea Shop Walks
Pub Walks along the Dorset Coast
Pub Walks in the New Forest

1st edition published June 2009

ISBN 978-1-898073-32-1

© Mike Power

Power Publications
1 Clayford Avenue
Ferndown
Dorset. BH22 9PQ
Powerpublications@hotmail.co.uk

Publisher's note
Whilst every care has been taken to ensure the accuracy of all the information given in this book at the time of printing, errors can occur dur to many factors. Paths are sometimes re-routed, stiles can replace gates and pubs regularly change hands. Neither the publishers nor the printers can accept responsibility for any inaccuracies.

Printed by: Pardy and Son
Photographs: Mike Power and John Quarendon
Front cover: The Walnut Tree, Appleshaw

INTRODUCTION

It is twenty years since I first wrote Pub Walks in Hampshire which was updated a few years ago and has been reprinted several times. I am happy to say it is still a popular book. Four years ago I planned a follow up but never quite got round to it as my time was spent travelling and doing other things. It was only when I spoke to John Quarendon, author of three of our very successful publications based in and around Surrey, who spurred me on and offered to walk or re-walk at least half of them. So together we have produced this new book of thirty more walks in Hampshire. This book in keeping with all others in the series are stitched bound with laminated covers.

John and I have our preferences as to what makes a good pub. Obviously it has to be a friendly and comfortable place to be in, offer a good range of well kept real ale and provide good home cooked food at an affordable price. The location is important ideally a village setting surrounded by open countryside. A tall order one might say but happily they do still exist and we have found some. As publishers we like to point out that no payment whatsoever is requested for inclusion in our books, they are selected by the authors on merit.

The walks vary in length from 2 to 5 ¼ miles and all start and finish at a pub. Where possible we suggest alternative parking but when limited to the pub only we would ask you seek permission first and obviously visit the pub on your return. Whilst opening times are published it is often best to telephone first just to make sure the pub is open. Each of these walks are accompanied by a sketch map which is not necessarily to scale but can act as a guide only.

The Rights of Way Act, which came into force on August 13th 1990, has much improved the rights of ramblers, it was a massive step forward in path protection. The Act requires occupiers who disturb the land to make good the surface within 24 hours of the disturbance or 2 weeks if the disturbance is the first one for a particular crop. Where no width is recorded the minimum for a path must be one metre and two metres for a bridleway.

It is always advisable to have with you an Ordnance Survey map, suitable weather proof clothing and well treaded boots. Where there are no pavements always try to keep to the right hand side facing the on coming traffic. It is useful to carry a stick to aid walking, clear brambles, test the stability of the ground ahead and which can be waved to deter animals.

Keep to the countryside code. Do not light fires, fasten all gates, and keep dogs under control and always on a lead where livestock are present. Take your litter home and do not pick or dig up wild flowers.

Due to the economic climate of today many business are struggling to survive none more so than pubs. It is a fact that one closes everyday so they all need our support. We hope in our small way we may have helped a few. We enjoyed these walks we hope you will too.

HAMPSHIRE

Map of walk locations

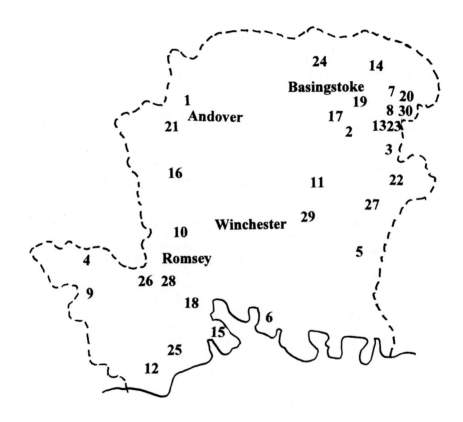

The Walnut Tree, Appleshaw

The Walnut Tree inn dates back to 1890 when it was called the Bell Inn. There are photographs on the wall showing how it looked at that time. The then landlord came to an untimely end when he was murdered by two men for his wallet; fortunately they were caught and hung. Set back from the main village road it is separated by a small ditch and grass area where some picnic benches are positioned. It is a lovely friendly village local with a small carpeted lounge and a larger dining room on the left both heated by open winter log fires. There is more seating outside on the sunny front terrace. Plus a secluded back garden for children

The inn is owned by Admiral Taverns and very well run by licensee Tony Burden Three well kept real ales include the lovely Timothy Taylor Landlord, Courage Best Bitter and Harveys Sussex

Food is served 12 - 2pm and 7 - 9pm. Snacks include cheesy chips, toasted sandwiches, hot baguettes, jacket potatoes and battered fish and chips. The main menu lists soup, semi coarse country pate followed by an 8 oz rib eye steak, a rack of lamb, lamb shank braised in mint sauce or red wine and rosemary, pork braised in cider and apple sauce, beef medallions in horseradish and juniper berry sauce. Also Cajun chicken breast, and vegetarian options - pasta tuna bake, vegetable lasagne verdi and macaroni cheese. Plus traditional favourites like cottage pie, traditional sausage and mash and liver, bacon and onions. Sweets to die for include bread and butter pudding, spotted dick, treacle sponge and chocolate waffle meltdown with fresh cream or ice-cream. Sunday roast lunchtime only 12 - 2pm.

Open everyday 12 - 3pm and 7pm - till closing, Sunday all day. Closed Tuesday. Families welcome.

Telephone/Fax: 01264 772626

Village signed from the A342 between Andover and Devizes.

Park at the front of the inn or in the lane.

Approximate distance of walk: 5¼ miles. OS map Landranger 185. Ref. 304/489.

A lovely walk from this most attractive of Hampshire villages. There are few stiles and the going is mostly flat and good underfoot on field and woodland paths plus well surfaced bridle tracks.

1. Leave the pub turning right and just beyond the last dwelling, but before reaching the wide grass verge lined with walnut trees take the sign-posted footpath on the right. Go up to the gate and across the field to the stile and squeeze gate beyond then down the field to one last stile turning left into the lane.

2. Walk to the end of the village, cross the road and join the sign-posted bridleway track opposite. After passing beneath the power lines take the track on the right which rises beside the power lines then bears left and right before reaching the tarred lane. Turn right and further on cross the road by St Margaret's Chapel and in a few paces down the lane join the grass track on the left. Keep beside the hedge until you enter an open field then turn right walking to the bottom and join the narrow path on the left which leads to the lane.

3. Turn left, go past the last of the farm buildings then fork right off the road and pick up a narrow footpath. Often muddy at first it borders a field before entering a bluebell wood. Turn right at the track and follow it as it merges with a tarred lane finally entering the pretty village of Penton Mewsey.

4. On the right look for a sign-posted bridleway, follow it up to the fingerpost and turn right along the narrow track, out to the lane and turn right. Walk until you reach the footpath on the left. It is signposted but can be concealed if the hedge becomes overgrown. Keep to this well maintained field footpath across to the stile, straight ahead on to the grass path, which runs beside a bluebell wood, through the kissing gate and up to the road.

5. Walk straight across to the signed footpath opposite and after entering the small wood turn left walking for a short distance until you see an exit on the right (not signed) follow the field path down to Ragged Appleshaw turning left into the lane and up to the stile on the right. Climb over retracing your steps back to the pub.

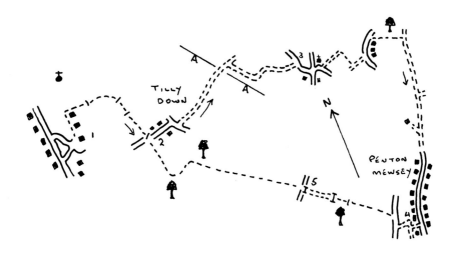

The Bull Inn, Bentley

The Bull is a most attractive pub inside and out and one can only imagine how much more relaxing it must have been before the A31 became a dual carriageway, with traffic passing close by at high speed. Fortunately the raised patio is comfortably above the traffic. There are comfortable low beamed bars either side of the entrance and on a busy Sunday the general hubbub easily drowned out the traffic noise.

The ales are Ringwood Best, Timothy Taylor Landlord, Youngs and Courage Best and there is an impressive wine list.

A printed menu gives a wide choice of pub grub, many dishes with an individual twist. Home-made burgers include venison with brie and redcurrant and Cajun chicken with goats' cheese and red peppers. The ploughman's come with home-made onion marmalade, plum chutney, salad and crusty bread. There is home-made soup of the day and a choice of omelettes, "Bull platters" to share and sandwiches on white or brown bread, baguettes or tortilla wraps. The specials cover a large blackboard. How do you fancy a starter of seafood knickerbockers glory topped with Bloody Mary ice cream? To follow there are steaks from the chargrill, pork fillet Wellington, sautéed lambs' kidneys and a mouth watering list of fresh fish dishes, e.g. seared king scallops, line caught sea bass and wild sea trout with samphire.

Children are welcome everywhere, well behaved dogs in the 'Regulars' bar only to the left of the entrance.

Opening hours are 10.30am - 11pm daily with food served Monday - Saturday from 12 - 2.30pm and 6.30 - 9.30pm, Sunday 12 - 8.30pm.

Telephone: 01420 22156

The pub is located above a lay-by on the eastbound carriageway off the A31, at a minor crossroads, 1½ miles east of the village of Bentley.

There is ample parking at the front in the car park and lay-by.

Approximate distance of walk: 3½ miles. OS map Landranger 186. Ref. 803/445.

A safe and very pleasant ramble across field paths to Alice Holt Forest returning through a SSSI, noted for wildflowers and butterflies, recrossing the River Wey and finishing on the St Swithin's Way. Birdworld Zoo is close by - go to the end of Gravel Hill Road and turn left.

1. Turn right out of the inn then very carefully cross the A31 dual carriageway into Gravel Hill Road opposite. Cross the bridge Over the River Wey, go past Bentley Mill then climb the stile into the field on the left. Head straight across the field passing between the lone oak and the stream, then through trees to a stile. Rein in the juveniles and dogs and carefully cross the railway line and stile following the gently rising path, bearing right onto a grass track and out into the lane. Turn left uphill and at the brow take the wide track on the right that leads to a barrier beyond which keep to the main track through the forest with fine views to the right in places.

2. You reach a narrow surfaced crossing track with an attractive pond to the left. For a short cut you could turn right here signed to Bentley Station - see dotted arrows on map.

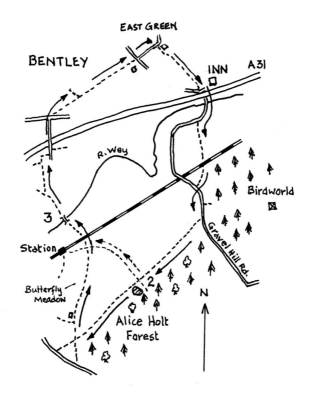

River Wey

Those interested in wild flowers and butterflies should continue on the main track for another 650 yards to reach a sign-posted crossing track. Turn right here and immediately fork right on a narrow path into woods. The path bends right then left to a kissing gate with Bentley Hall to the left. Turn right here into Bentley Station Meadow, a SSSI particularly noted for butterflies, also moths and glow worms for any who walk by torchlight. In a few yards, at a fork keep ahead right and follow the well walked grass path (short cutters rejoin the walk here) and in a few yards re-cross the railway line and a stile. The path leads to a stile onto a drive, where go straight ahead between cottages to another stile then follow the waymark across a field to a footbridge over the River Wey, we were 'buzzed' by a low flying buzzard here.

3. Continue on a path between hedges and at a fingerpost go ahead through a metal gate and along a fenced grass track to reach a farm. Turn right at the first fingerpost, then in 20 yards at the next one turn left over a stile into a field. Walk up the field and turn right through a gate to pass behind the house

to a stile and on to a bridge over the A31. Cross the bridge and at a T junction turn right. In 50 yards bear left to two stiles in a field. Follow the waymark arrow towards a large oak, maintaining direction into the field ahead, down to a small bridge and up to a stile. At this point you join the St Swithin's Way and to welcome us in 2008 the farmer had ploughed up the footpath. Your way is straight across to a waymark post and a gate that gives access to a large field divided into fenced horse corrals. Follow the waymark through gates and over stiles until you have the farmhouse on the right. The direction of the waymark arrow across the last field is misleading and it may be best to follow the right hand edge of the field beside the farm drive to a stile on to a lane. You could turn right down the lane back to the pub. Alternatively cross the lane and go forward to the attractive first house in the hamlet of East Green. Turn right across the grass in front of it and through a hedge tunnel to a stile into a field. Keeping close to the hedge walk down to a kissing gate and a path that leads back to the pub.

The first house in East Green

The Cedars, Binsted

The Cedars is a typical small village pub serving the local community with welcoming staff, two bars one reserved for dining with bright gingham tablecloths and a central fireplace that serves the two rooms. Small it may be but it certainly attempts to punch above its weight with beer festivals, live music, a bouncy castle and playground in the large rear garden and a very extensive menu.

The ales are changed regularly and are advertised in advance. On our visit the choice was Jennings Cockerhoop, Bateman's XB, Skipton's Copper Dragon, John McGuinness and Moondance from the local Alton Brewery.

Pub favourites appear on the printed menu with a wide selection of hot baguettes and baps, sandwiches on white or brown bread served with chips and a side salad, choice of jackets and ploughman's, three egg omelette, 8oz 'Cedar' burger with Aberdeen Angus steak topped with cheese, bacon and egg. Sunday roasts are popular and booking is recommended. There is much more on the blackboards, e.g. Thai red curry, sweet and sour chicken, lamb kofta, paella and crusty bread, coconut breaded butterfly prawns and chicken and porcini stroganoff.

Children are actively encouraged and dogs are welcome except in the dining room.
Opening hours, Monday-Friday 12 - 2pm and 6 - 11.30pm. Weekends open all day.
Food service: Mon - Sat 12 - 2pm and 6 - 9pm, Sunday 12 - 7pm.
Telephone: 01420 22122

The small attractive village of Binsted can be reached from the A31 at Alton. It is signed from the roundabout west of the town.

There is ample parking at the pub.

Approximate distance of walk: 3½ miles. OS map 144. Ref. 744/410.

An extremely enjoyable, peaceful and scenic walk on good paths and tracks that pass beside a series of picturesque ponds and skirts the small hamlets of South Hay and Wheatley. Going is generally good underfoot - but could be muddy in places during the winter.

1. Leave the inn turning left and just beyond the high wall take the signposted footpath left, which leads to the Holy Cross Church and the village centre. Dating from about AD1140 the church is one of the oldest in Hampshire. To their great credit the management have allowed four swallows nests in the porch roof despite the mess they have made. All the while the brave Mediterranean hunters continue to shoot our migrating birds we cannot allow one nest of those who make it here to fail. Field Marshal the Viscount Montgomery of Alamein, who lived at Isington Mill nearby, was buried in the churchyard on the 1st April 1976. Go through the churchyard to the far back right-hand corner passing Monty's grave and through a gap into a field and straight ahead to a grass crossing track. Turn right then

quickly left towards the wood on the far side. Drop down the path to a plank bridge, then up steps to a grass track and turn left. This track soon narrows to a grass path following the tree lined valley and passes between a series of ponds and open fields. Continue until you reach a crossing track with a metal gate barring your access to the last and largest pond, now a nature reserve.

2. Turn right on the track and in a few yards at the waymark bear left up steps into a field and continue along the left hand edge. Reach a fingerpost on the left that leads you down steep steps that may be perilous after rain and across the valley bottom to a concrete bridge. Cross into a field and bear slightly left at first then, with trees in front of you, bear slightly right and steeply uphill along the left-hand edge of the field. At a fingerpost in

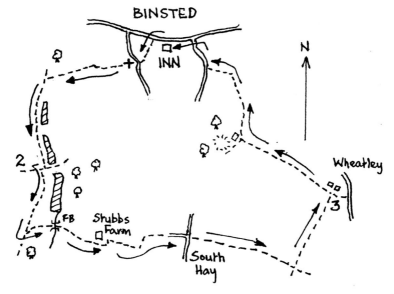

front of a barn turn left into Stubb's Farm, then turn right on the farm drive which leads to South Hay. At a village road go straight across to the track opposite that leads to a couple of fields separated by two stiles, then on a narrow field path. After about 600 yards at a waymark post turn left along the edge of the field on a narrow path that eventually becomes a track into Wheatley.

3. Do not turn right down to the village but turn left in front of the first house you come to and through a gate onto a wide track between fields. Keep to the right of an old building with a disused quarry to the left and the track reaches a lane, where turn right then left at the T-junction and back to the pub.

One of the Ponds on the Nature Reserve

Stubb's Farm near Binsted

The Bat & Ball Inn, Breamore

Nestling in Hampshire's Avon Valley the Bat & Ball, originally built some 250 years ago, lies between Salisbury and Ringwood in the delightful village of Breamore. The village dates from the 16th century with an ancient manor house and Saxon church surrounded by many chocolate box cottages. It is a popular haunt for fishermen having access to the nearby River Avon.

The Inn recently changed hands and at the time was nicely refurbished to a high standard. A "good pub" competition run by Hampshire Life Magazine placed the inn in second place. A comfortable, part boarded and carpeted dining room has a mix of tables and chairs and a fireplace which serves both this and the central bar area. There is a separate locals' bar at the opposite end and ample outside seating in both the nice garden and on the smart terrace

The well stocked bar has a good range of drinks including three real ales, presently Sharp's Doom Bar, Adnams Broadside and Courage Best.

Very good food, sourced locally wherever possible, is served Monday to Saturday 12 - 2.30pm and 6 - 9pm, Sunday 12 - 8pm. There is a diverse mix of modern and traditional international dishes ranging from Thai curries to Italian risottos. The ever changing menu includes fish dishes and a variety of game, meat and vegetarian meals. Plus the usual bar snacks.

Children and dogs are equally welcomed.

Weekday opening times 12 - 3pm and 6 - 11pm, Sunday 12 - 10.30pm.

Telephone: 01725 512252, Fax: 01725 510980. www.thebatandball.com

Walk No. 4

Pub located in the lovely village of Breamore on the B3078 between Ringwood and Fordingbridge.

Parking available at the pub or opposite in the village streets.

Approximate distance of walk: 5¼ miles. OS map Landranger 184. Ref. 159/178.

A fairly long but extremely enjoyable level walk which takes you first across fields to the Countryside Museum, Manor House and Saxon church. Breamore House completed in 1583 was built for the Dodington family but later purchased in the 18th century by Sir Edward Hulse and has changed little over the years. (It is open to the public Easter weekends also Tuesday, Wednesday and Sunday in April. Tuesday, Wednesday, Thursday, Saturday and Sunday between May and September and every day in August 2 - 5.30) The second half of the walk takes you over farm land before crossing the River Avon returning through Woodgreen along peaceful country lanes. Although not over demanding the areas close to the river can be very wet in the winter.

1. Carefully cross the road turning right and almost immediately turn left into the lane. Go up past the school, into the field on the right and straight ahead passing close to the cricket square making for the right-hand side of the large house. Walk to the corner and join the grass path leading to the stile. Go up the field to the next stile, cross and keep straight ahead to the stile in the far hedge, go out into the lane and turn right.
2. There are some pretty estate cottages along the route as you head towards Breamore House. At the bend turn right then left onto the wide gravel track past the Countryside Museum. (Opening times 1 -

5.30) Go through the courtyard to the track and turn right walking as far as the church and head up towards the front porch. Dating from 980 AD little is known until 1130 after which it was administered by the Augustine Priory, once located north of the mill. Take the path on the right which leads to the kissing gate then keep straight ahead in the direction of the waymark to the stile in the fence. Take time to look back at the lovely view of the house. Maintain direction to the stile in the fence opposite and continue towards the small wood making for the gate on the left. Almost immediately go into the wood on the right following the little path

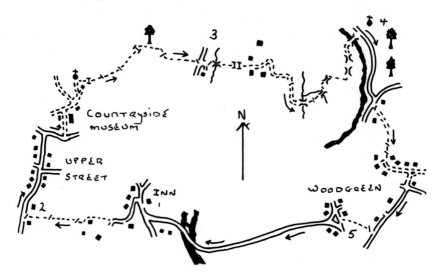

16

Church at Breamore

Mill on the Avon

which leads to a stile. Climb into the field bearing left and negotiate a couple more stiles before reaching the road.

3. Carefully cross to the sign-posted path opposite following it over the stile and plank bridge, across the field to the kissing gates and straight ahead through the farm, and out to the track. After rounding the dwelling, the track reaches a stile on the right. Follow the track beyond and when you reach the bridge cross into the field on the left then turn immediately right making your way over the grass to the stile and plank bridge. It can often be very wet here in winter, waterproof footwear essential. Keep to the fence, cross the next bridge and stile and turn right. Keeping close to the right-hand hedge boundary walk almost to the bottom of the field turning left when you see the plank bridge. The track beyond passes over another small bridge before reaching the Avon river

Cross to the far bank, go up to the lane and turn right.

4. Follow this peaceful lane up to the junction, turn right then cross the lane and join the sign-posted Avon Valley Footpath. Go up the short track then keep to the boundary on the right, over the stiles and up the track forking right at the junction. After merging in front of the Green keep straight ahead on the tarred road and when almost on the far side climb the stile on the right located just beyond a seat. Go down the path to the bottom and out into the road by The Horse & Groom, an excellent refreshment stop.

5. From the pub turn left then take the lane on the right sign-posted to Breamore. It is fairly peaceful but can carry some traffic at certain times. Its very scenic where it crosses the Avon by the mill. Upon reaching the road simply turn right a short distance back to the pub.

Breamore House

The Five Bells, Buriton

The Five Bells is a welcoming village pub with a saloon bar, a dining room, a public bar and a snug each with a log fire in winter.

Hall & Woodhouse owned the ales are Badger and Tanglefoot with Hopping Hare, Sussex and Fursty Ferret as seasonal variations.

Food service is Monday - Saturday 12 - 2.30pm and 6.30 - 9.30pm, Sunday 12 - 3.30pm. At the weekend sandwiches are available in the afternoon up to 5.30pm. Menus are changed regularly and may feature local meat and game including pan fried Buriton pigeon breast - wood pigeons are advised to steer clear of the fields hereabouts - crab and watercress tart, calves liver and bacon, sirloin steak with warm onion marmalade and moules mariniere served Belgian style with chunky chips, chilli and coriander. Specials may include fisherman's pie and steak, Guinness and oyster pie. There is a choice of roasts on Sundays frequently featuring "Mr Johnson's Buriton pork" from a local farm. The sandwich menu is unusually enticing, e.g. brie, rocket and balsamic strawberries, fresh Devon crab and watercress, English rare sirloin and horseradish and there is a good choice of ploughman's and salads.

Children are welcome and dogs in the public bar and the grassy rear garden.

Opening times are 11.30am - 3pm and 5.30 - 11pm, weekends open all day.

The pub has two self-catering rooms in a separate building.

Telephone: 01730 263584

Walk No. 5

Pub peacefully located in High Street, Buriton best reached from the A3 south of Petersfield.

Park at the pub or in the roads close by.

Approximate distance of walk: 3¾ miles. OS map Landranger 197. Ref. 737/203.

A very enjoyable walk high into the Queen Elizabeth Country Park. Strenuous in places it is mostly on well surfaced paths and tracks.

1. Leave the pub walking down through the village, past the pond to the church then bear right following the track round to the stile on the right. Bearing slightly right walk up the field to the stile in the top boundary and simply follow the path beyond which rises fairly steeply through deciduous woodland interspersed with the occasional yew tree. Garlic ransoms and dog's mercury dominate the woodland floor in springtime

2. Upon reaching the drive turn right onto the South Downs Way, walk to the junction and go straight ahead, through the car park to Halls Hill and gate opposite. The route takes us up this wide gravel track until we turn right at the cross track. Further on fork right to join the slightly narrower track which rises gently then flattens before dropping down through beautiful scenic woodland. Ignore the footpath on the right but continue all the way down and round until you reach a signed-posted footpath on the left. Climb the stile and bear right to a second then follow the gully down the hillside to the stile at the bottom and turn left onto the track which takes us up to the lane.

3. Turn right and, safely keeping to the right-hand side, go over the railway bridge walking until you reach the bend then cross over to the sign-posted footpath on the left. Keep to the field path beyond the stile maintaining direction to three more stiles before reaching the road where we turn right back to the village. For a slightly picturesque extension to the walk you can turn left into Bone Lane which leads to the church.

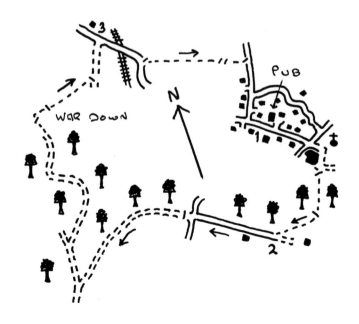

Buriton Pond

The Jolly Sailor, Bursledon

Situated on the edge of the Hamble overlooking the marina the lovely, atmospheric Jolly Sailor is reached by a footpath from the very pretty village of Old Bursledon. Customers come from all round by car, train and boat to enjoy the excellent fayre or just sit with a drink and take in the view. Two front rooms which overlook the water have bow fronted windows, boarded floors, an open fireplace and walls adorned with nautical regalia. There is very atmospheric dining room with a mix of high pew seating and solid chairs and tables. The heavily flagged-stoned rear bar has a wealth of old beams and timbers. On fine days the most coveted seats are on the the narrow waterside terrace but there is also a covered summer dining area on the jetty. The cool flower filled rear terrace has a mix of large heavy tables interspersed with patio heaters for those cooler days or nights.

The pub is owned by Hall & Woodhouse offering a range of their excellent real ales like Tanglefoot and Fursty Ferret.

Very good well presented food cooked to order is served every day between 12 and 9.30pm. The set menu lists dishes such as charcuterie a selection of fine Italian meats topped with pesto, peperonta - a combination of peppers, tomatoes, mozzarella, fresh basil with plenty of garlic, a trio of sausages and lime and coriander chicken salad. Fish lovers can choose from moules mariniere and a fantastic fish pie (their words). Vegetarian dishes might include roasted pepper pasta and a roasted vegetable goats cheese tart.

Families welcome up to 9pm dogs allowed on leads but not in the dining areas
Opening times all day every day 12 - 11pm.
Telephone: 023 80 405557

Pub located in Lands End Road, Old Burlesdon. Can be reached from road on the A3025 or A27, by train or by boat.

Parking is very restricted outside the inn better try and leave your car in the village or at the railway station.

Approximate distance of walk: 4¼ miles. OS map Landranger 196. Ref. 490/095.

An interesting and enjoyable walk, generally good underfoot which, apart from the historic village of Old Burlesdon and a busy road junction, is entirely on well-surfaced, rural, field and woodland paths.

1. From the pub we turn right, cross the railway bridge then turn left up High Street through lovely Old Burlesdon. Carry on past the viewpoint which overlooks Hackett's Marsh, turning left at the junction. Keep straight ahead at the junction of Kew Lane and almost immediately join the signed footpath on the left at the side of the ineptly named 'Thatched Cottage'

2. Follow this well maintained footpath eventually reaching the lane at the bottom. A few paces further on take the signed footpath, down between the dwellings on the left. Cross the steam and head up the track leading to Mallards Moor, an attractive strip of broad-leafed deciduous woodland. Near the top fork left to the concrete road, turn right and then left onto the signed footpath beside the high wire fence.

3. Walk until you reach a small path on the right then go up to the road and turn right.

Carefully cross the busy junction turning right and then left into Hound Road. On the left is the church of St Mary the Virgin dating from 1230. Next to the church there is an ecology park with well-marked paths and a seat to rest awhile.

4. Cross the road and join the footpath on the right then almost immediately bear right beside the hedge to reach a stile. Climb the rise and follow the path beside the hedge, past the lake and onto a track which leads to the road. Turn right; go straight over Hamble Lane and down the path between the houses leading to a cul-de-sac. Continue straight ahead down through the estate eventually reaching the playing fields. Bear right to the bottom staying close to the stream until you reach a gravel path and bridge on the left.

5. Go up to the lane and cross to the path opposite climbing to the lane at the top. Turn right and soon join the signed footpath on the

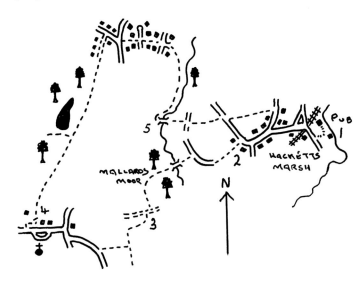

left. Upon reaching the lane turn right walking past the chapel of Our Lady of the Rosary. Greyladys was originally the home of Mrs Emmaline Shawe-Storey who had the chapel built in 1906 and opened for public use by all the Catholics in Burlesdon. Turn left at the next junction retracing your steps back to the pub.

Viewpoint over Hackett's Marsh

St. Mary the Virgin

The Foresters Inn, Church Crookham

Cheerful young staff welcome you into the handsome and spacious Foresters, originally two foresters' cottages. Much is made of the forestry theme with log piles outside and in and a log arch over a log burning stove.

The management declares that they serve unpretentious home cooked food cooked with flair. It seemed like a fair claim and the menu is extensive. There is a good choice of sandwiches, wraps and ploughman's and niceties like antipasto, crispy dipping mushrooms and Japanese style torpedo king prawns. More substantial fare includes on the menu a recommended wine to complement each dish. Choose from the likes of souvlaki kebabs, assorted steaks, calves liver and bacon, chef's fish pie, pork loin with caramelised apple and Kobi steak burger with all the trimmings. A specials board has daily extras, usually including fresh fish and there is a choice of roasts on Sundays, for which a blackboard exhorts you to "Come early, when it's gone it's gone".

Children are welcome but no pushchairs in the pub please. Dogs are welcome in the large sunny garden and in the uncarpeted bar areas outside of food service times.

Opening hours are Monday - Saturday 12 - 11.30pm, Sundays 12 - 10pm.

Food service is 12 - 3pm and 6 - 9.30pm, Sundays 12 - 8.30pm.

Telephone: 01252 616503. info@foresters-dining.co.uk

Walk No. 7

The Foresters is on Aldershot Road, about half a mile east of Church Crookham. It can be reached by turning south-west off the A323 between Fleet and Farnborough.

There is adequate car parking at the pub and opposite.

Approximate distance of walk: 4 miles. OS map 145. Ref. SU 826/527.

A most enjoyable walk with much of interest for all the family, crossing heathland used for vehicle testing by the military with views over Farnborough airfield and then along a section of the Basingstoke canal with much wildlife and through woodland.

1. Cross the pub car park to a gap in the hedge that leads to a kissing gate, where turn left on a path that runs parallel to the road. Soon reach a wide kissing gate and cross the road past a barrier and onto a track. In a few yards go over a cattle grid and on across the Long Valley heath, an area controlled by the military. You may encounter cattle grazing in the quieter sections. Paths here are too numerous to mention them all but cattle grids and notice boards make adequate reference points. Go over two crossing paths and your track curves left, now with Tweseldown racecourse on your right. Wildlife watchers should look out for deer, stonechats, Dartford warblers and a host of dragonflies. Go through a kissing gate and over the crossing track beyond. At the next crossing track turn right. At the next crossing track turn right. Go over a cattle grid, then turn left and immediately left again onto a very wide sandy track. There may be fine entertainment for men and boys here as you may see military vehicles racing up and down over the ruts and puddles. The safest, flattest path is probably on the right hand side of this track. At a wide crossing track go straight on passing a blue and while Test Traffic Direction sign on your left. Keep to the left over another crossing track and, with Farnborough airfield visible ahead, as the tracks bear right look down left for a narrow track guarded by a metal pole barrier with a danger notice beyond. Take this sunken path to a 'T' junction where turn right. You should now be able to see the spans of Eelmore Bridge at 10 o'clock and that is your destination. The path runs above the A323 and is, incidentally, a superb free vantage point to see the Farnborough Air Show. After a sharp rise and fall turn left at a 'T' junction with a surfaced track, cross the A323 and the Eelmore Bridge and turn left along the Basingstoke Canal towpath.

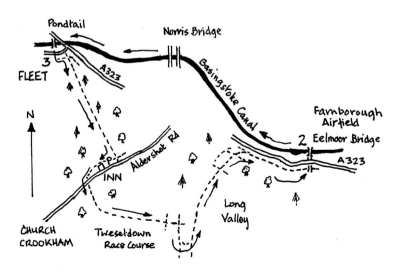

2. You are on this path for the next one and a third miles along a pleasant section of the canal with plenty of interest in water birds, wild flowers, blackberries in season and particularly fish. The water is clear enough to see pike lurking and any amount of smaller fry. You go under the two high spans of Norris Bridge and then reach Pondtail Bridge, another double. Go under the first that carries the A323 into the Fleet then turn up right and cross the second bridge to reach a road, where cross over and turn left.

3. Just before the 'T' junction turn right on a path into woods. Go through a wide kissing gate and ahead on a track, initially through a short avenue of pines, then on for half a mile ignoring side paths. Just before a 'T' junction with a car park to the right turn right on a path with the car park fence on your left. Go over a crossing track and in about 150 yards turn left through a kissing gate back in the pub car park.

Pike in the Basingstoke Canal

The Plume of Feathers, Crondall

Crondall is a picturesque village and the striking Plume of Feathers sits on a prominent corner site with tables along the frontage. The original building dates back over 500 years and it has been an inn for at least 370 years and maybe more. The interior walls were wattle and daub, the upper storey jettied out over the ground floor and the roof was thatched. Oliver Cromwell stayed here on the 8th October 1645 (Crondall was a roundhead stronghold at the time) before visiting some pain on Royalists at Basing House. A framed history is on the wall in the bar. Today it is one of those delightful village pubs that those of us less blessed would love to move to our own locality. Exposed beams, a log burning stove and a warm welcome set the tone in the small front bar.

This is a Greene King house and the greatest compliment I can pay the brewery is that the pub feels like a freehouse. Only the choice of ales reveals the connection - IPA and Old Trip with a guest, Everard's excellent Tiger.

Food is served from 12 - 2.30pm and 7 - 9.30pm, Sunday 12 - 3pm and 6.30 - 8.30pm. The bar menu, all on blackboards, has a selection of sandwiches and baguettes e.g. BLT, club sandwich, pork and leek sausage, chicken liver pate. There is a choice of ploughman's and tuna melt on open ciabatta. More substantial fare includes home-made 'Plumeburger', chicken Caesar and Greek salads, chicken and ham pie, koftas with tzatziki and salad. The cosy restaurant at the rear has a big fireplace now fitted with a gas fire. The separate menu here offers some serious cooking such as crayfish and asparagus tartlet with parmesan crust, pan fried dorado fillet, filo parcel filled with Mediterranean vegetables and feta cheese, Dover sole and supreme of chicken sautéed with tomato and grapes and a choice of steaks with a choice of sauces.

Children are welcome, dogs on the front and rear patios only.

Opening hours are 11am - 3pm and 6 - 11pm, Sundays 12 - 10.30pm.

Telephone: 01252850245

Odiham Castle

Old cottages in The Borough, Crondall

Walk No. 8

Crondall can be reached from Junction 5 of the M3 via the A287 for 4 ½ miles, then turn south at the sign, or from the A325, West Street, in Farnham, where turn west on Crondall Lane for 3 miles. At the T-junction in the village turn left and The Plume of Feathers is on the left.

The car park is behind the pub, entrance in Church Street.

Approximate distance of walk: 4¼ miles. OS map 144. Ref. SU 745489.

An excellent exercise walk for all the family, mostly on good tracks with fine views, bluebells in season, deer and a historic church.

1. Turn left out of the pub and admire the cottages opposite before turning left in Church Lane where there are more cottages. At the T-junction in front of All Saints Church turn right into Croft Lane. There has been a church on this site since the 9th century and it was mentioned in the Domesday Book in 1086. It has been rebuilt over the centuries and in 1659 a new tower was built modelled on a church in Battersea and the result is an imposing edifice that has been called 'the cathedral of North Hampshire'. Close inspection will reveal much of interest including three crusader crosses, a 14th century memorial brass and a 'momento mori' of a skeleton and shroud. A pamphlet detailing the history is for sale in the church. Continue along the lane past Farm Lane and at a sharp right hand corner go forward on a waymarked track towards barns and keep to the track as it turns left in front of the barns. Stay on this path between fields then at a fork turn right to reach Lee Wood. You may well encounter deer here and certainly bluebells in season. Emerge from the wood and maintain direction along the right side of a field. Half way up the field fork right on to a stony track in a woodland strip. The track improves to pass houses and there is a view right of the twin humps of Horsedown Hill. Seeking confirmation from a local I was informed that he knew of no horses with feathers - he had called it TitsUp Hill for 50 years and was at a loss to understand why the Ordnance Survey had so far failed to adopt the descriptive superiority of his alternative.

2. At a T-junction with a lane turn left still going gently up hill. Just before a T-junction with another surfaced lane there is a fine view north down to Crondall Church and beyond. Turn left and you are now on The Harrow Way, a very ancient track way across the North Downs that becomes the Pilgrims' Way in Surrey. The view south to the right should convince you that England is still 'a green and pleasant land'. Eventually your long gentle climb reaches a summit and you start an equally gentle descent.

3. Reach a fingerpost on the left and turn here beside a gate on to a grass track with Barley Pound Wood on your right. Further on a gate on the right gives access to a track leading to the site of a 12th century ring motte and bailey fortification in the woods, believed to have been at one time the stronghold of local outlaws. Returning to the track, continue to a junction, where turn right on a signed footpath along the left hand side of a field. At the end go to the field corner and turn left through a waymarked gap then up the field edge to a waymarked T-junction. Turn left through a hedge tunnel and past back gardens to emerge at the corner of the churchyard, where go forward on Church Lane back to the pub.

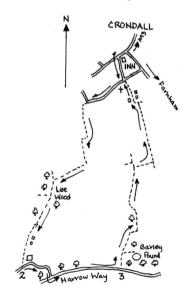

The Compasses, Damerham

Find The Compasses and you've found one of the best. Dating back over 400 years the inn was at one time virtually self sufficient with its own dairy, butchery and brewery, the old brew tower still standing. The inn overlooks the cricket green and acts as a focal point for village life. Perfect for walkers the cosy public bar has bare wood floors, a pool table at one end and padded, pew seating at the other end perfectly positioned to enjoy the warm log winter fire. There is a small lounge bar a comfortably furnished dinning room and recently added smart rear conservatory. There are eating areas in the delightful front and rear gardens.

Ownership of the inn changed recently and is now in the hands of Enterprise Inns and extremely well run by the new licensee Linda Lamont. The well stocked bar offers a large choice of malt whiskies plus four real ales, Marston's Pedigree, plus local brews Ringwood Best Bitter and Forty-niner also Hop Back Brewery's Summer lightning.

Imaginative food is available Monday to Saturday 12 - 2.30pm and 6.30 - 9.30pm, Sunday 7 - 9pm. Prepared from the freshest ingredients there is a set menu from which you can choose ploughman's or sandwiches plus starters like salmon and dill fish cakes and pigeon breast served on rocket salad followed by steak and kidney pudding, smoked haddock and prawn fish pie and medallions of pork with bubble and squeak, beetroot puree and caramelised apple. Several dishes are chalked daily on the blackboard plus a range of puddings like syrup sponge and crème brulee.

Families welcome, dogs allowed in public bar

Opening times 11 - 3pm and 6 - close. Sunday all day 12 - close.

6 en-suite rooms all individually decorated with TV and coffee making facilities.

Telephone: 01725 518231 Linda@compassinn.uk.com

Allen River

Village signed from Sandleheath off the B3078 3 miles north from Fordingbridge.

Ample parking at the inn also outside in the road.

Approximate distance of walk: 4 miles. OS map Landranger 184. Ref. 105/161.

A fairly long but enjoyable walk mainly on wide open field paths and bridleways.

1. Leave the pub and go down West Park Lane opposite walking to the lane junction then continue ahead on the track, footpath signposted. Upon reaching the track junction turn right walking to the top of the rise then fork left and continue on beyond the gate. At the cross track turn right, go to the top, climb the stile into the field and turn right.

2. Keeping close to the right hand boundary walk to the corner of the field then turn immediately left, and with the hedge to your right go up the rise and down. Continue down beyond the gate to the track and turn right then left at the gate and almost immediately climb the stile into the field on the right.

3. Cross both stiles then maintain direction down the larger field to the gate in the corner, across to the small stile finally down to one last stile and turn right. Continue along the field boundary and after passing the farm buildings, turn right and go up the field. Part way up, enter the field on the right, turn left and continue ahead. At the end of the hedge bear slightly left down to and through the gap in the hedge following the slightly raised grass path ahead, which passes beside a waymark sign and leads to a stile. Continue ahead until you reach the end of the hedge at which point fork slightly left, up and over the rise to the stile, out into the lane and turn right.

A short distance down the hill join the signposted footpath on the left which passes through a narrow strip of woodland then bears right across the field to a small wood before reaching the village. Turn right back to the pub.

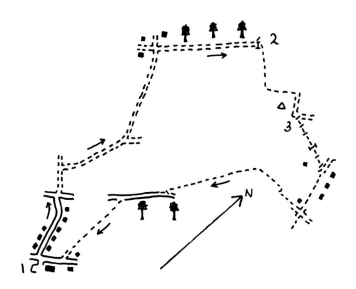

The sketch maps in this book are not necessarily to scale but have been drawn to show maximum amount of detail.

The Mill Arms, Dunbridge

The Mill Arms is an attractive two storey 18th century former coaching inn set in the heart of the Test Valley. Close by is Mottisfont Abbey famous for its rose gardens and the Howard Hillier Arboretum. Surrounded by flower filled gardens the inn is conveniently situated right opposite the railway station. The interior has retained many of the original features; bare boarded and flagstone floors, oak beams and large open fireplaces with a nice assortment of chairs, tables and sofas. There is a skittle alley perfect for functions. The pub owns a mile stretch of double bank fishing on the River Itchen below Bishopstoke.

The inn is a freehouse offering an excellent selection of wines and real ales

Food is served everyday, lunchtime 12 - 2.30pm and evening 6 - 9.30pm, all day Saturday 12 - 9.30pm and Sunday 12 - 9pm. All the food is home prepared and cooked to order, the inn priding itself on not buying in ready meals. Apart from traditional bar food like home-made lasagne and home baked ham, the changing daily specials, 5/7 starters and 9/12 main courses could include salmon fish cake with poached free-range "Claytons" egg , hollandaise sauce and grilled courgettes to a Jerk spiced breast of Gressingham Duck with endive, sweet potatoes dauphinoise and redcurrant jus. For vegetarians there might be grilled asparagus tagliatelle, tomatoes and herb cream. What better way to finish than with traditional favourites like sticky toffee pudding, rhubarb crumble or double chocolate brownie with Baileys ice cream. Sunday roast with a smaller child's portion.

Families welcome.

Opening times Monday - Friday 12 - 2.30pm and 6 - 11, Saturday all day 12 - 12pm, Sunday 12 - 11pm.

6 en-suite rooms one with a four poster.

Telephone: 01794 340401.   Fax: 01794 342281 millarms@btconnect.com

Come by road. Village easily reached from the A3057, Romsey to Stockbridge road at the Mottisfont turning. Come by train station opposite.

Car park at the front and rear also limited space in the road.

Approximate distance of walk: 5 miles. OS map 185. Ref. 319/261.

A lovely peaceful walk through woods, on field paths, along peaceful country lanes which twice crosses the River Dun.

1. Leave the pub turning right then go right again into Russell Drive. Walk up the hill, onto the gravel track and fork right over the stile and follow the track ahead through the bluebell wood. Keep to the main track and continue ahead, beyond the stile follow the well defined grass track which leads to a stile in the wire fence. Turn left, cross to the stile opposite keeping straight ahead beside the wood then bear right at the corner and follow a line beside the wire fence on the right leading to a stile. Walk to the top of the field, then straight ahead down the other side to the stile turning right into the lane.

2. Walk for a short distance, cross over and join the sign-posted footpath opposite. A couple of stiles lead to a small path, another stile taking you into a field. Keep straight ahead to a fourth and staying close to the hedge on the right walk down to the lane and turn right.

3. Take the next turning left and go up the hill walking as far as the gravel track on the right. Take care as you share this with trucks before reaching the yard. Bear left at the yard towards the way post sign and turn right taking the narrow path up the hillside looking for the exit to the lane before reaching the barn at which point we turn right. Keep to this extremely peaceful lane, past Chapel Farm and the old cemetery, walking until you reach the stile on the right before the bend. Bearing left cross the field to the stile in the wire fence maintaining direction to the stile by the trees. The path beyond winds down through a small wood to a stile after which bear half left, down the field to the stile, out to the lane and turn right.

4. Upon reaching the village of Butts Green, and at the junction with Cooks Lane, keep straight ahead past the Kings Arms then take

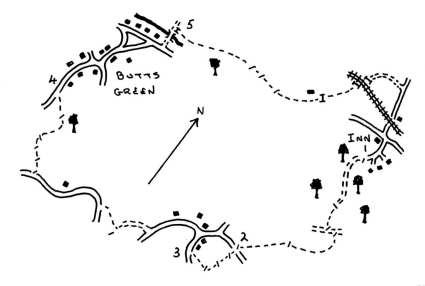

Walk No. 10

the next right into Butts Green. Walk down to the road, turn right, and in seventy or so paces, cross over to the gravel track following the footpath sign over the bridge.

5. Immediately go through the kissing gate on the right following the well beaten path across the meadow - a picture in summer with numerous wild flowers and butterflies.

Cross both stile and plank bridge and continue in the direction of the waymark. The easy to follow path takes you over more stiles at one point passing beside some very remote cottages before reaching a gate. Continue ahead then carefully cross the railway line, go up to the road and turn right back to the pub.

River Dun

Village Pond, Hartley Mauditt

The Three Horseshoes, East Worldham

At first sight the Three Horseshoes looks more like a small hotel than a village pub and indeed they do have four letting rooms. Inside the building's age is revealed by a fine old fireplace, one of three in the dining areas around the bar.

On our visit in August 2008 new managers in this Fullers house had only been in situ for two weeks but had certainly hit the ground running. Five ales were on offer Chiswick, London Pride, HSB, Adnams bitter and Qucksilver from Osset in Yorkshire. They had their menus printed and emphasised that they obtained all their meat from a local farm and their vegetables from a local market, the theory being that if they obtained their supplies from the same place as their local customers they could not go far wrong. Certainly the local produce and excellent cooking we sampled suggest that they have a winning formula.

Food service is daily 12 - 2.30pm and 6.30 - 9.30pm, except Sundays. The bar menu has a good choice of sandwiches, jackets, baguettes, hot melted baguettes and home made soup of the day. Main courses include local pork and leek sausages, home made pie of the day, home-made lasagne, beef burger and vegetable and mozzarella burger. Blackboard specials were paella, lamb jalfrezi and gilt head bream with orange and onions and there is a whole lot more on the a la carte menu all at prices that provide excellent value for money. The locals are indeed fortunate.

Children are welcome in the pub and in the attractive garden with a brick barbecue and view of the thatched cottage next door. Dogs also, except in the dining areas.

Opening hours are 11 - 3pm and 6 - 11pm.

Telephone: 01420 83211

Walk No. 11

East Worldham is on the B3004, Cakers Lane, 2 miles east of Alton. The Three Horseshoes is on Cakers Lane at the junction with Blanket Street.

There are car parks at the front and back of the pub.

Approximate distance of walk: 3¾ miles. OS map 133. Ref. SU 747/381.

A pleasant walk among arable fields with fine views in places passing through the ancient village of Hartley Mauditt with its Norman church, scenic pond and buried tragedy. Nettles may be a hazard in season at the end of Section 1.

1. Cross the front car park and the end of Blanket Street and soon turn right up steps to a stile into a field. Keep beside the hedge on the right and cross a stile to enter an enclosed path. Cross a lane and maintain direction on a grass track opposite. Just past the field opening on your right turn sharp left on a path with a row of trees on your left. At the end follow the direction of a fingerpost to turn right still with trees on your left. Maintain direction along the field edge through a gap in the hedge and under power lines. At the next fingerpost bear left into the trees then right on a narrow path downhill. Cross a waymarked stile by a gate into a field and turn right to another gate and out on a track that bears right uphill. Cross a tarmac lane onto a track and in a few yards take the narrow footpath to the right of a metal gate.
2. Reach a double gate and turn right onto a surfaced lane uphill. At cross roads turn right signed to Hartley Mauditt. You soon reach the village pond, a delightful spot and very popular with anglers. On the left is the simple Norman church of St Leonards beyond which is the site of the buried medieval village of Hartley Mauditt, supposedly abandoned after the plague decimated it inhabitants in the 14th century. There are nice views to the left as you progress toward West Worldham.
3. As you enter the village note the Victorian post box in the wall of The Wren's Barn. There are lavender fields in this village and bushes all along the side of this house welcome you with sight and smell. In a few yards, where the road turns sharp left, cross to a stile by a gate and head up a field bearing slightly right to a double stile in a fence. Continue on the well walked path across fields, stiles and footbridges and under power lines to a gap in trees. In the next field go forward on a grass track with trees on your left. Where the trees end bear half right across the field towards the left hand side of a group of barns. Turn right on a surfaced lane and in 100 yards bear left on the footpath you started on and back to the pub.

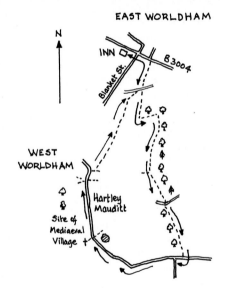

EAST WORLDHAM

N

INN

B3004

Blanket St.

WEST WORLDHAM

Hartley Mauditt

Site of Mediaeval Village

The sketch maps in this book are not necessarily to scale but have been drawn to show maximum amount of detail.

The Crown Inn, Everton

"No strangers here only friends we've yet to meet"

The greeting on the front wall of this very attractive gastro pub which has circular picnic benches at the front interspersed with tree ferns and other interesting plants. This warm friendly village inn has recently been taken over by Janine and Phil who were previous owners of Rouille Restaurant in Milford on Sea. Since taking over they have refurbished the inn in a modern contemporary style complementing the old with the new.

The bar is fairly small the rest given over to dining.

All the food is home made except the bread. Served daily 12 - 2.30pm and 6pm till late, Sunday 12 - 3pm and 7pm till late, typically you can order fishy starters like pan-fried scallops, mussels cooked in garlic and cream or asparagus and oyster mushroom salad. Tempting mains include liver and bacon, half a shoulder of lamb and pork medallions followed by sticky toffee pudding, pan fried banana in butterscotch sauce and strawberry cheesecake.

Opening times: - Monday to Saturday 11.30 - 3.30pm and 6 - 11pm.

Sunday 12 - 4pm and 7 - 10.30pm.

Telephone: 01590 642655. info@crown-inneverton.co.uk

Walk No. 12

The pub is located at Everton and conveniently signed a short distance back from the main A337, New Milton to Lymington road.

The inn has its own car park at the rear but there is ample parking in the road outside.

Approximate distance of walk: 2¼ miles. OS map Outdoor Leisure 22. Ref. 293/942.

A short but very enjoyable ramble commencing on a country lane and track culminating on a meandering path through a delightful wood before returning along the lane. Ideal for all the family.

1. Walk back to the main A337, cross over at the refuge and turn right. Turn left at the junction into Lymington Road then left again into Lymore Lane. Go past Braxton's Gardens unless you wish to pay a visit. They specialise in herbs and David Austin roses, then fork left walking until you reach the gravel track on the left. Footpath is signposted.

2. Continue beyond the gate and at the sharp right-hand bend go straight ahead into the field. Bearing hard left walk towards the corner where a short way back you will find a path which winds its way through a small attractive area of wet woodland crisscrossed with streams and ponds and home to bluebells, primroses and other springtime flowers.

3. At the finger post turn right keeping to the path over the stream, around the field, back into woodland and up a grass track, onto a drive and beyond into Agarton Lane. Fork right at the junction then right again through Lymore passing as you go some very smart country dwellings and a few pretty cottages. Simply follow the lane back, past Braxtons Nursery, retracing your steps to the Crown.

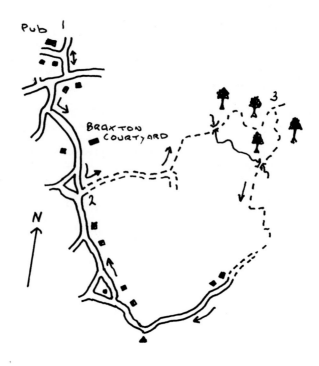

The Fox & Goose, Greywell

A flight of steps lead directly into the bar of this lovely 16th century village local which has a dark green painted ceiling, an assortment of simple furnishings and bench seats positioned on the red quarry tiled floor to make the most of the stove in the large inglenook fireplace. There is a dartboard on one wall together with various interesting regalia. Mandy's fresh laid eggs can be purchased at the bar "get a dirty dozen" The other bar is carpeted with dark furniture, a heavily beamed ceiling and big fireplace. A large field at the back has picnic benches with a children's play area.

Up to five real ales are usually available which might include Batemans XXXB, Gales, Courage Best, Abbot Ale and Wadworth 6X plus a 14 bin wine list.

A varied food list is available weekdays 12 - 2.30pm and 6 - 8.30pm, 9pm Friday and Saturday and Sunday 12 - 5.30pm. On my visit I noticed a board listing a choice of 9 or 12 inch pizzas with your own choice of toppings whilst the bar menu listed the usual snacks like sandwiches, baguettes, toasties and filled jacket potatoes. The main menu starters range from garlic mushrooms to crispy Camembert followed by breaded scampi and lemon sole, lasagne, mixed grill, various steaks, a mega sized cod in batter and ham off the bone with egg and chips. Sweet lovers can choose delights such as spotted dick and chocolate pudding. More choice is listed on the specials board and on my last visit offered smooth Ardennes pate, breaded seafood platter, cannelloni, real butcher's faggots with mashed potatoes, a sausage platter consisting of Hampshire pork with leek and wild boar and home-made corned beef hash. There is a Sunday roast plus speciality cream teas served in the afternoon.

Children welcome. Dogs in bar only on a lead.

Weekday opening times opening times 11 - 11pm, Sunday 12 - 10 30pm.

Telephone: 01256 702062

Walk No. 13

The village is easily reached from junction 5 off the M3. Take the A287 south and Greywell is signed immediately on the right as you leave the exit roundabout.

There is a large car park at the rear of the pub.

Approximate distance of walk: 2¾ miles. OS map Explorer 144. Ref. 718/514.

A lovely walk at first along the towpath of the Basingstoke canal to the ruins of Odiham Castle and then across an area of Wadborough Green before entering attractive woodland. The final part follows a field and fenced path leading down to the pub. Although a touch hilly the walk is not over demanding but can be a bit wet in places. Boots are essential in the winter months.

1. From the pub turn left, them immediately right into Deptford lane and in a few paces join the footpath on the left signposted 'to the Basingstoke Canal. Cross the bridge and turn right onto the canal towpath. The bridge is the end of the Greywell Tunnel, 1230 yards long and built between 1788 and 1792. There was no room for horses so the barges had to "leg it" lying on their backs and pushing with their feet against the tunnel roof, which could take up to 6 hours. The tunnel collapsed and is no longer open for traffic but has been taken over by colonies of four species of bats. Follow the tow path to the ruins of King John's Castle, from whence he rode out to sign the Magna Carta at Runnymede in 1215. Continue a short way to a kissing gate, where turn left across a field and car park to another kissing gate that leads to a lane. Turn left and keep to the left

past two fords across the River Whitewater. Then turn left over a cattle grid into a short residential road. Go to the end and out through a small gate. Bear slightly right and then pick up a path through an area of Wansborough Greens. This path may be a bit muddy in places. The area is managed by the Hampshire Wildlife Trust with the aim of restoring grazing and traditional usage.

2. Leave by the stile and cross the road to the sign-posted path opposite. Beyond the stile the path goes through a small copse then crosses the end of the road to enter the wood opposite. Ignore the 'private' sign, the waymark is on top of the gatepost. At a fork keep right. Generally good underfoot the track makes its way through this delightful wood before a waymarked post directs you to the left. In a few yards at the next waymark fork right through mixed woodland keeping

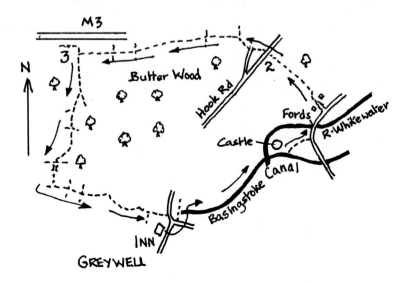

Basingstoke Canal

to the wide grass path past three waymarks until you reach a T junction with a wider path and fence beyond.

3. Turn left and at a waymark post fork right on a wide grass track between coppiced hazels. Go over a waymarked crossing track and at a T junction turn right and at the next T junction with a wide grass track turn left downhill. At the bottom of the hill is another T junction go straight ahead onto a narrow waymarked path into woods. Cross a concrete sleep bridge and at a T junction turn left. Go over two crossing tracks and up a rise to a waymarked gate. Pass through and turn immediately right to a waymarked post in a field. Go ahead to another post, then bear half right to a stile in the bottom right-hand corner of the field. Turn right on a fenced path that leads you down to a road, where turn right back to the pub.

The ruins of King John's Castle

The Shoulder of Mutton, Hazeley

According to their card "The Shoulder of Mutton is a traditional 18th century English country inn located in the quiet village of Hazeley Heath", so quiet that it does not merit a mention as such on the OS map. They seem to think that the village is called Hazeley, but either way it is very small so it is surprising that it can support such an excellent hostelry, converted to an inn from two 14th century cottages. As you enter it ticks all the boxes: a warm welcome from friendly staff and in winter from a log burning fire in the bar and another log burning stove with copper cowl. The attractive décor is all exposed beams and brickwork, brass and copperware, pretty curtains and banquette seating by the windows. Outside there are a couple of patio areas leading down to a grassy garden with nice views over cow pastures.

The ales are Hog Back T.E.A, Adnams' Bitter and a guest, Bombardier on our visit

Food service is 12 - 2.30pm and 6 - 9.30pm. The bar snack menu had all the usual items at prices that seemed reasonable given the quality of the ingredients. "Proper" ham was promised and delivered. The main menu features fresh fish like king scallops and bacon, roast monk fish, lemon sole mornay and fresh mussels plus a good meat selection of fillet steak, sirloin, T bone and gammon steaks. Pork medallions, half a roast duck, chicken wrapped in bacon and surf and turf - sirloin with scampi and prawns. Vegetarian dishes include mushroom stroganoff, risotto, cannelloni, vegetable stir fry and a selection of appetising salads. Sunday roasts are popular.

Children are welcome and dogs in the central bar area and the garden.

Opening times: 12 - 2.30pm and 6 - 11pm.

Telephone: 01189 326272

Walk No. 14

Hazeley straddles the B3011 about 2 miles north west of Hartley Witney. The pub is on the Mattingley road just west of the junction with the B3011.

There is a car park at the side.

Approximate distance of walk: 5¼ miles. OS map 144. Ref. SU 743/590.

A pleasant walk over farm land with bluebells in season, fallow deer and buzzards circling overhead. You cross the River Whitewater twice and visit an unusual brick and timber church.

1. Turn left out of the pub and up to the B3011, cross over and continue past the bus shelter. Now look for a stile at the end of the wooden fence on the left. Cross here and continue with a fence on your left to another stile, then maintain direction along the field edge to another stile. Turn left on the track which narrows to a waymarked path and in a few yards keep ahead left at a fork down through a small bluebell wood and on to a footbridge, then between fences. Cross another footbridge over the rather pathetic River Whitewater and turn right along the fence and on to reach the B3349 by Hound Green Garage. Turn left then right onto Vicarage Road. Ignore the first fingerpost on the left and continue to the second, which is hidden behind a small oak tree opposite a house with tall Elizabethan style chimneys.
2. The sign points directly across the field to a copse but the path, ploughed over in 2008, lies half right to the very far corner of this long field about 500 yards away. There is a way through into the next field. Turn right along this meadow to a footbridge in the left-hand corner and on up to a waymarked stile. Keep beside the left-hand hedge over two more stiles then along a fenced path and out onto a gravel track. Advance to the road and cross to the fingerpost opposite then down through a woodland strip to another wood where turn right then bear left into Mattingley village. Bear right to the church. The interesting brick and timber building started life as a meeting hall and so has no patron saint a real life 'St Elsewhere'. The bricks used in the herringbone design were especially made in the parallelogram shape locally on the Hazeley Estate.
3. Enter the churchyard and bear left to a footbridge and kissing gate, turn right down a farm track, then left through a wide pair of gates. Cross a concrete bridge into a field and bear slightly right towards the fenced River Whitewater. Turn right along the fence to a kissing gate and plank bridge, then onto a waymarked narrow concrete bridge and a plank bridge. There was a mill here at one

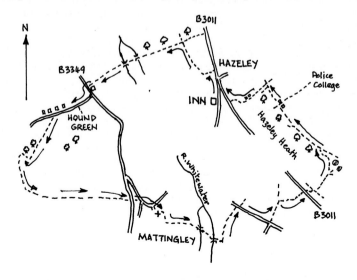

46

time but the site is not properly visible from the path. Cross the field ahead and turn left in front of the hedge. In the corner negotiate two stiles and a plank bridge then head across a meadow to a kissing gate, after which turn right on a lane. Ignore the first fingerpost on the left and after passing two houses turn left at a fingerpost onto a grass path that soon widens to a track. After about 200 yards look for a path going right. The fingerpost was missing in 2008 but there are a couple of yellow arrows as you progress. The path meanders up through trees and eventually meets a gravel drive that leads you out to the B3011.

4. Cross over to the narrow path opposite that leads to onto Hazeley Heath. At a 'T' junction turn right and at a fork go left. At a fork under telephone lines go left and at the next fork go left again, soon passing ponds

over to your right. Now bear right to join the boundary path next to the ditch and hedge. At a fork keep right down to the ditch. Look out for fallow deer before you reach the grand lodge entrance to Bramshell Police College. Cross the drive and take the footpath left that soon widens to a track through the woods. At a path junction take the second path left, signed "footpath no horses". Pass some cottages on your right and continue up a wide grass path. Ignore a waymarked post that seems to have been turned to cause confusion and bear right past a house onto a gravel drive. Where it bears left go into the trees on the right to pick up the little path which drops down steps to the road. Follow this left past Hill Farm and out to the B3011. Turn right carefully along the gravel verge to the junction, where turn sharp left back to the pub.

Mattingley Church

The Bridge Tavern, Holbury

Situated on the edge of the Forest the Bridge Tavern dates back to 1750 and last changed hands in 2002 at which time it was refurbished to a very high standard by Maggie and Ady. Beyond the entrance porch there is a locals bar on the left, warmed by an open log fire having bare brick and half timbered walls, board floors and assorted furnishings. The beautifully appointed dining area has bare brick walls supporting a heavily beamed and timbered ceiling creating a comfortable ambience. Outside there are two enclosed gardens.

A good range of drinks presently include a couple of real ales, Ringwood Best and Wychwood Hobgoblin.

Good home cooked food, prepared on the premises, is available weekdays 12 - 2pm and 6 - 9pm, Sunday 12 - 3pm and 7 - 9pm. There are speciality home made pies along side the regularly changing blackboard specials which might include lamb chops with redcurrant and rosemary, beef balti, Cumberland sausage with mashed potatoes and onion gravy, stir fried chicken with cashew nuts and prawns plus veggie dishes like spinach, cherry tomatoes and mozzarella pudding and mushroom stroganoff. Monday night is curry night and Thursday big steak night. Chef's treats and cream teas.

Children welcome, dogs in public bar only.

Opening times 12 - 2.30pm and 6 - 11pm. All day Saturday and Sunday.

Telephone: 023 8089 2554. www.thebridgetavern.co.uk

Ipers Bridge lies on the Holbury to Beaulieu road close to Fawley best reached from the A326.

Good sized car park with some limited parking outside.

Approximate distance of walk: 2 miles. OS map Outdoor Leisure 22. Ref. 032/424.

A short but enjoyable ramble ideal for all the family. Not demanding the route is on a mix of tracks and forest paths at one point crossing a small stream. Summer is probably best as the paths and tracks can sometimes be very wet and muddy.

1. Turn left out of the pub, up the hill and left through the gate beside the cattle grid. Continue along the edge of the heath until you reach the well surfaced track on the left. Just before reaching the inclosure turn left onto the narrow path which runs close to the wire fenced boundary, dips to a bridge then bears right to a second. After crossing the stream keep straight ahead until you reach the cross track and turn right.

2. Stay on the path which rises to a wide track between two copses. Be warned it can be muddy. Maintain direction through a half timbered gate then go straight ahead, past farm buildings on the left keeping to the track which bears to the left before reaching the hamlet of Roughdown.

3. Go past all the dwellings and just before reaching the cattle grid take the green lane track on the left, often uneven and muddy. Turn right at the cross track, down to Rollestone Road finally turning left along the grass verge to the pub.

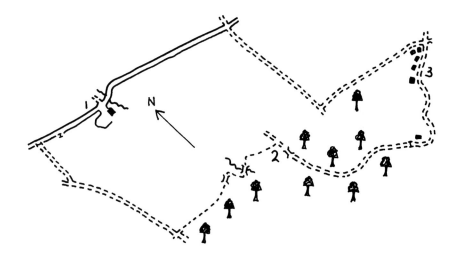

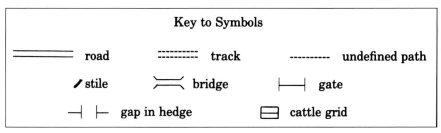

Key to Symbols

——— road	---------- track	---------- undefined path
∕ stile	⊃—< bridge	├——┤ gate
┤ ├ gap in hedge	⊟ cattle grid	

John of Gaunt Inn, Horsebridge

Situated beside the River Test this charming white painted inn is a picture bedecked with flowers in summer. A great village local from the front one enters directly into the lovely L shaped bar having country style furnishings on a carpeted floor.

The well stocked bar offers three real ales Palmers IPA, Ringwood Best and Fortyniner plus Thatcher's dry cider and a good selection of wine.

Food is served Tuesday to Friday 12 - 2.30pm and 6 - 9.30pm Saturday 11 - 3pm and 6 - 9.30pm, Sunday 12 - 3pm. All home-made and freshly prepared, blackboard listed starters range from garlic mushrooms and fried brie to fresh olives with feta and warm bead. There is a good range of fresh salads such as Caesar, avocado, bacon and brie, a three mixed seafood and ham ploughman's. From the main blackboard menu I noticed steak from a local butcher together with a trio of award winning sausages cooked in rich onion gravy plus moussaka, lasagne and chicken, broccoli and Stilton home made crust pie served with mash and peas. Naturally fresh river trout also features on the menu. How could you not choose a sweet the only problem, which one? Jamie's home-made chocolate ginger nut slice, dark rich plum pudding, spotted dick, syrup sponge, or chocolate indulgence. Children's menus are available at half price. Tea is served in the afternoon. Wednesday night is curry night. Saturday, between 6 and 9.30, you can eat as much pie and mash as you want with a free half a lager or a pump soft drink, priced in 2009 at £8-96. Booking essential. Sunday roast.

Opening times Monday 6 - 11pm Tuesday 12 - 2.30pm and 6 - 10pm Wednesday to Friday 11 - 3pm and 6 - 11pm, Saturday all day 11 - 11pm Sunday all day 12 - 10pm.

Children and dogs welcome.

Telephone: 01794 388394

To reach Horsebridge from Romsey after about 5 miles turn off the A3057, Romsey to Stockbridge road at the brown information board, pub signed ½ mile.

Ample parking around the pub. In the small car park at the rear or opposite in the Test Way car park.

Approximate distance of walk: 3 miles. OS map Landranger 185. Ref. SU 346/304.

A lovely level walk along the Test Way crossing the river several times. It is easy going suitable for all members of the family.

1. Leave the inn and turn right, cross the bridge and join the sign-posted, Test Way on the right. This well surfaced track, fringed in springtime with clumps of primroses, was once a branch railway line. It crosses a tributary of the Test before reaching The Clarendon Way. Either side of the track are numerous may trees, blackthorn and elderberry, a kitchen paradise for the birds in the autumn.

2. At the Clarendon Way turn left following this wide, well surfaced gravel track which thrice crosses tributaries of the River Test, home to numerous waterfowl before reaching the road at Houghton. Although not busy it is best at first to keep to the wide grass track on the left thereafter cross to the right hand side for safety. Walk as far as the junction then turn right.

3. After crossing the brook the road climbs gently under a leafy canopy, on the left are three delightful Elizabethan houses. On the right are two pairs of houses, almost opposite is a wide, well surfaced gravel track (footpath is sign-posted). Go down and once more cross two more sections of the Test before reaching a stile. Climb into the field and bearing left walk to the stile on the far side, and re-join the Test Way. The path bears to the left passing the Horsebridge Station which now operates as a tea room, open certain times in the summer. Turn right on the other side of the station and walk straight up the lane back to the pub.

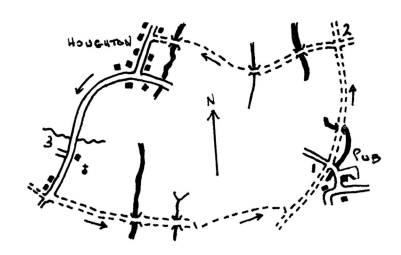

The sketch maps in this book are not necessarily to scale but have been drawn to show maximum amount of detail.

River Test

Horsebridge Station

The Four Horseshoes, Long Sutton

The Four Horseshoes, a free house, is an absolute gem; the perfect village pub, beautiful inside and out with sumptuous hanging baskets in summer and cosy with two log fires in winter. There is a central bar adorned with shining brassware and collections of mugs from around the world. Rooms either side of the bar and a front conservatory offer dining options. The landlord, from Yorkshire, is the chef and his menu, all on blackboards, is enticingly priced and has been well thought out. Fish dishes predominate with tuna, cod, plaice, hake, scampi and salmon all featured. Other offerings include steak and kidney pudding, mignons of lamb, sausages and mash and 'Portobello' casserole of steak in red wine. The ploughman's are outstanding using proper cos lettuce and succulent local ham with none of the usual shower of makeweight leaves that would give any self respecting ploughman apoplexy. You get a warm Yorkshire welcome and the cooking is superb, all excellent value for money.

The ales are an esoteric collection, as befits a free house, and include some new to me e.g. Scatter Rock Guzzler and Somerset Cottage Brewery's Reservoir Dogs. You may also find Palmer's Dorset Gold or Triple FFF or Moondance from the local Alton Brewery.

The garden across the road is literally a field with a well equipped children's playground and a petanque court (boules available). There are three letting rooms for B & B and campers may pitch their tents on the field. Dogs are welcome in the central bar.

Opening times are 12 - 2.30pm and 6.30 - 11pm. Food is served from 12 - 2pm daily except Monday and Tuesday and 6.30 - 8.45pm except Sunday.
Telephone: 10256 862488

Walk No. 17

Long Sutton is signed to the west from the B3349 between Odiham and Alton. Go through the village passing the church on your left and the pub is about half a mile along Wingate Lane on the right.

There is ample parking opposite the pub.

Approximate distance of walk: 4½ miles. OS map 144. Ref. 748/471.

An enjoyable easy going walk through the grounds of Lord Wandsworth College and along a byway, then passing by the well at Well and finishing over field paths with fine views. Expect mud in winter.

1. Turn right out of the pub and right again into the main entrance the Lord Wandsworth College, a boarding school founded in 1914, originally for orphans, subsequently extended to single parent children and eventually to fee payers. Whatever their circumstances they are fortunate to enjoy a superb setting and extensive sports facilities here. Progress up the drive to the zebra crossing and bear right on a tarmac path that cuts the corner. Cross at the next zebra and turn right, then take the left turn that leads to the visitors' car park. Go ahead through the car park and turn right on the footpath between the sports fields. Reach a road and cross to a small car park. Continue ahead through a waymarked gate, pass a vertical railway sleeper and go straight down the field to a hedge at the bottom. (The O.S. map shows a diagonal path to the bottom hedge but the field has been ploughed up and the waymarks show the route to follow.) Turn right at the hedge and after 150 yards go through a gap in the hedge and turn left on

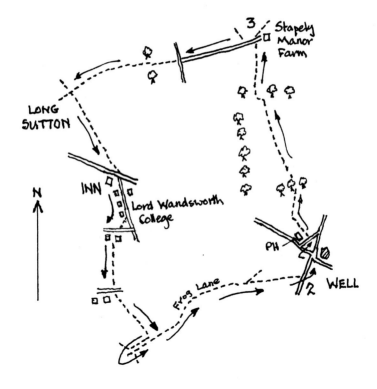

Frog Lane. This rough track is your route for ¾ mile. Grin and bear it and look out for the bird life. We saw goldfinches, bullfinches, willow warblers and a buzzard overhead.

2. Reach a surfaced lane and turn left to the village of Well. At the cross roads turn left past the well, gifted to the village by the Lord of the Manor in 1888, even though it had been in use for centuries beforehand since, like the Four Horseshoes, it stands on the ancient Harrow Way, which in Surrey becomes the Pilgrims' Way. Shortly you reach another attractive pub, The Chequers, notable for its vine covered patio. Turn right here and about 50 yards past the pub car park turn left over a stile and go ahead across a small field to another stile and maintain direction to a third stile. Here your route lies diagonally right following the waymark arrow. Care may be needed here as the farmer tends to plough up and plant over footpaths. Aim for a spot to the right of an indentation in the tree line ahead where a stile is concealed. Cross and maintaining direction follow the waymark arrow across another field to a waymarked small gap in the trees. Now with a hedge on your right go ahead up the field to reach a lane.

3. With Stapley Manor Farm to your right turn left on the lane. At a 'T' junction cross into the field opposite and maintain direction down the field, through a gap in the hedge and straight on down another field. In the middle of the field turn left on a crossing path to reach a stile. Stay close to the hedge following the path out into the lane where turn right back to the pub.

The Well at Well

Waterloo Arms, Lyndhurst

Peacefully situated on the edge of Lyndhurst lies a hidden gem the very atmospheric Waterloo Arms. Dating from the 17th Century it is a traditional 2 storey thatched inn. From the front one enters directly into the low, heavily beamed main bar which has an assortment of tables and chairs. A comfortable red sofa is conveniently situated next to one of the two open fireplaces which house warm winter log fires. The central bar serves both the main bar and cosy rear dining room beyond which is a large attractive rear garden with tables on the rear terrace and a lawned, flower filled garden.

The well stocked bar has good real ales which on my last visit included Adnams Broadside, Sharp's Doom Bar and Ringwood Best.

Food is excellent all freshly prepared and cooked to order using locally sourced ingredients where possible. Available everyday 12 - 2.30pm and 6 - 9pm Monday - Thursday and 12 - 9pm Friday, Saturday and Sunday. There are snacks of filled baguettes, jacket potatoes and a salad bowl with Ciabatta. The extensive, constantly changing menu could list smoked fish chowder or a brie pot - Port and walnuts caramelised in the oven and served with red onion relish. Board specials on my last visit included beef Wellington, whole tilapia stuffed with coconut rice and chicken julienne with tarragon, pan fried and served on a bed of cucumber and saffron with a white wine sauce plus a vegetable lasagne. Of the 7 or 8 tempting sweets how could one choose between crème brulee, apple and rhubarb crumble or even a Mars bar and brandy mousse. There is a children's menu, offering tasty sausages with bubble and squeak and ham, egg and chips plus a daytime salad buffet between 12 and 6pm plus a Sunday roast.

Pub open all day.

Families welcome.

Telephone: 023 8028 2113. www.waterlooarmsnewforest.co.uk

Located in Pikes Hill just outside Lyndhurst off the main A337, Lyndhurst to Cadnam road.

Large rear car park and 'on road' parking at the front.

Approximate distance of walk: 4 miles. OS map Outdoor Leisure. Ref. 298/087.

A lovely mostly level walk across open forest and through attractive inclosures. It is generally good underfoot but can be wet in places during the winter.

1. Go back down the road keeping to the right-hand pavement then carefully cross the busy A337 towards the telephone kiosk opposite and walk a short distance down Racecourse View. Pass through the gate on the left and head across the lawn towards the small bridge. Follow the path ahead up through the copse and onto the golf course. Keeping an eye out for stray golf balls bear right following the wide grass area making for the far wood. Look for the large wide track, if you miss it walk along the boundary to the right. Once found follow it to the bridge keeping to the path ahead, cross the track and continue ahead on the small winding path between a mix of beech, oak, holly and birch trees before reaching the cross track.

2. Turn left here keeping to the track which eventually reaches open heath. Stay on the path ahead which eventually bears to the left, rises through birch trees then drops down to a gate.

3. Turn left, then once more carefully cross the A337 to the gate opposite and enter Foldsgate Inclosure. Forking left make your way across the grass towards the wooded area then keep straight ahead to the far corner where a path enters the wood which consists mainly of holly trees. Further ahead the path rises past an enclosed field on the left then bear left to meet the lane.

4. Keep straight ahead towards the cattle grid and just beyond go down the track on the left past the dwellings to the gate and turn right across the grass leaving by the gate opposite. Close by is the source of the Beaulieu River. A few steps furter on turn right in front of the house, "Woodside" and go along the path, named "The Lane" then turn left at the road walking the short distance back to the pub.

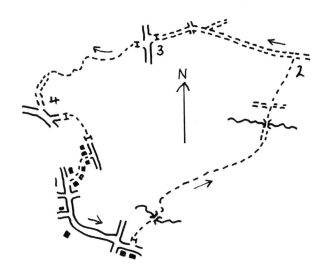

The sketch maps in this book are not necessarily to scale but have been drawn to show maximum amount of detail.

The Gamekeepers, Mapledurwell

Remotely situated this delightful 19th century rural country inn is popular with diners from miles around. Inside there is a flagstone floor and beamed ceiling, it even has a well inside.

Owned by the Dorset Brewers, Hall & Woodhouse the inn offers an interesting range of good wines plus five real ales which presently include Badgers First Gold, Tanglefoot, Sussex Best, Fursty Ferret and Stinger.

Food is served both lunch time and in the evening. For those just wanting a snack there is the usual pub fayre, ploughman's, jacket potatoes and sandwiches and favourites like steak and kidney pudding or cod in beer batter. But for serious dining starters range from devilled kidneys sauté in cayenne pepper, Worcester sauce, onions and mushroom cream served on toasted croutons and fresh mussels cooked with chillies and coriander to gravadlax on fresh blinis, mixed leaves, lemon and dill creme fraiche to whole Turnworth cheese, honey and thyme glaze, home-made plum chutney served with fresh bread for 2 to share. Heading the list of main meals is a chargrilled fillet of beef, blue cheese and pink peppercorn butter, dauphinois potatoes with baby spinach, cherry tomatoes and red wine jus. There is also pan fried calves liver, and pan fried sea bream fillets, char grilled sausages and confit of duck leg cassoulet, Toulouse sausage and butter beans served with fresh bread. Game and daily fish specials plus a range of home-made desserts.

Opening time 12 - 3pm and 5.30 - 11pm, Saturday and Sunday all day 11am - 11pm.

Children and dogs welcome.

Telephone: 01256 322038. www.thegamekeepers.co.uk

Mapledurwell is easily reached from Junction 5 of the M3. Take the A287 south and follow the sign for Greywell found immediately on the right as you leave the exit roundabout. After 2 ½ miles Mapledurwell is signed on the left. After ½ mile at the village centre turn immediately right into Tunworth Road and The Gamekeepers is on your right.

There is ample parking at the pub.

Approximate distance of walk: 2¾ miles. OS map 144. Ref. 686/514.

An enjoyable easy going ramble for the most part on scenic field paths.

1 Turn right out of the pub and opposite the attractive Rye Cottage on the left turn right into the drive of The Old Chapel. There is a fingerpost but it may be concealed. Keep to the right and go through a gate and up to a stile. Bearing slightly right cross to the stile and plank bridge in the hedge opposite and turn left on a fenced path. Go through a gate and straight ahead across a grassy area to a gate. Cross the road to a kissing gate and finger post. Go up the field to a stile and maintain direction with a hedge on your left to reach another stile. Bear left around the perimeter of the field passing a waymarked gate on your left. In the bottom corner of the field there is a stile very well concealed in trees. Cross and turn right and right again on a lane.

2 Pass a dogs' graveyard on your left and just past a large barn on the left enter the second field on the right at a waymarked post. With the hedge on your right go ahead to a kissing gate then bear half left across the next field towards the hedge. In 2008 the path had been ploughed up and the stile removed, but persevere to find a gap in the hedge. Go through and turn right along the hedge and turn left on the track at the bottom. At the junction of 'Five Lanes' take the first turning on the right and stay on this field path which descends gently into a wood. The path runs close to the field edge on the right.

3 Look for a kissing gate and enter the field to join a raised grass path that leads through a gateway, now with a hedge on your left. Maintain direction through another gateway to reach a stile by a gate that leads to a fenced footpath to a lane. Turn left on the lane if you want to visit the church of St Mary the Virgin, which is sited near a spring in common with Celtic and Saxon tradition. Otherwise go ahead past the village pond into Turnworth Road and back to the pub.

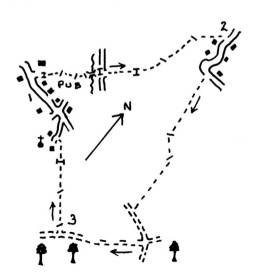

St Mary the Virgin

The Crown and Cushion, Minley

The old established Crown and Cushion began as a cottage built in 1512 and was converted to a pub in 1596. There is an interesting story relating to the naming of the pub concerning a failed attempt in 1671 to steal the Crown Jewels by one Captain Thomas Blood and, following his capture, the suicide of his mistress a Miss Cushenor Cussens. Her dive into Hawley Lake was tragically premature as Charles II unaccountably pardoned Blood.

Set side on to the road the pub has a nicely furnished long bar. Outside front and rear paved patios run the length of the pub and the adjacent function room Meade Hall. This authentic looking building was constructed in 1989 from materials salvaged from two 400 year old barns. At the back the patio is separated from a cricket pitch by a picket fence the battered condition of which may be testament to the power of the batsmen's straight driving.

A Shepherd Neame house the ales are Bishop's Finger, Spitfire and Kent's Best.

Bishop's Finger features in the batter on delicious fresh cod. The menu offers a selection of sandwiches on white or brown bloomer bread with home-made chips. Ploughman's and very appetising salads complete the cold fare. Main courses include calves liver and bacon, sirloin steak with all the trimmings, wild mushroom tagliatelle and green chicken curry. "Light bites" are available e.g. bubble and squeak with a fried egg, ½ pint of prawns, scrambled egg and smoked salmon. A regular special is a mixed plate of Thai starters for two to share.

Children are welcome, dogs in the garden only.

Opening hours are 12 noon to 11 pm daily. Food service is Monday-Friday 12 - 3pm and 6 - 8.45pm. Weekend 12 - 10pm.

Telephone: 01252 545253

Walk No. 20

Minley is hard to define. A manor, a wood, two farms and some cottages bear the name but mostly it is a barracks situated off the A327, which runs between the A30 south of Blackbushe Airport and Junction 4A of the M3. From the M3 follow signs for Reading and the pub is signed on the left after half a mile.

There is a large car park at the pub.

Approximate distance of walk: 3¾ miles. OS map Ref. SU 834571.

The walk circles Hawley Lake which is usually a hive of interesting activity with much bird life and human pursuits and also visits Hawley Mill mostly on bridleways and tracks through woodland. Close attention to route finding is recommended. The O.S. Map has failed to keep pace with the development of roads and tracks by the military. Bridleways and footpaths may have been widened to surfaced roads or tracks but the only military vehicle we saw was a security patrol and there appeared to be no impediment to quiet enjoyment of the area.

1. Cross the road from the pub and go through a gap in the hedge then turn left on a surfaced footpath. At a wooden barrier on the left turn right on a signed bridleway through woodland. At a crossing track turn right and look out for a low bridleway post on the right, where turn left. At the next marker post turn right through

rhododendrons to reach the shore of Hawley Lake. The large building opposite belongs to the Royal Engineers and to the north of this is the Sail Training School. There is much to see from the various access points to the lake shore. In addition to the sail trainees and canoeists there are some very sophisticated model boats. One angler was combining two

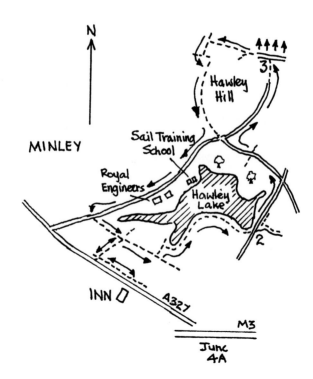

hobbies by sending his ground bait out to the desired location in a remote controlled powerboat fitted with a tipper bucket - much classier than a catapult. None of these activities seem to discourage families of swans, mallard, moorhen, grebes and Canada and greylag geese. Keep close to the shore through an area of soft sand that narrows to a path through more rhododendrons.

2. Reach a road to turn left on a bridge over an outlet from the lake. Continue on this surfaced road to a crossroads, where turn left on another surfaced road still signed as a bridleway. Go over a crossing track and at the next crossroads turn right on a surfaced road that leads up Hawley Hill. At the top is an extensive clearing. There was no sign of the Grand Old Duke of York but there is plenty of room up here for his ten thousand men to parade and about turn for the return march. You, on the other hand, can proceed bearing slightly left towards a line of trees.

3. Before reaching the trees turn left on a surfaced road that soon deteriorates into a track and at a fork keep right into woods. At the next crossing track turn left on a signed bridleway downhill and at a 'T' junction with another bridleway turn left. In 50 yards turn right at the next bridleway marker and at a fork keep right on a sandy track. Reach a crossroads with a surfaced road and turn right soon to pass through the STC and RE car park. Continue down the road past a speed hump and turn left to re-enter the MOD training area. At the fire crossing track turn right back towards the A327 and retrace your outward steps back to the pub.

Meade Hall at the Crown and Cushion

The Black Swan, Monxton

It is said Monxton has more thatched dwellings per head of population than any other village in England driving through it is not hard to see why. The Black Swan is thatched together with all the others in the terrace. A gem of a pub one enters through a low ceilinged, flag-stoned hall into the high ceiling, beamed bar. A couple of steps bring you to a cosy wood floored lounge with brown sofas positioned in front of the fireplace. A door leads out to the rear garden which has seating right down to the river. At the side are several comfortable dining areas once the stabling area for the patrons' horses.

Owned by Barron and Co Leisure well served real ales include Ringwood Bitter and London Pride

Food is served every day Monday - Sunday lunchtime 12 - 2.30pm, Monday - Saturday evenings 6 - 9.30pm Sunday 7 - 9pm Takeaway fish and chips Monday - Saturday 6 - 7.30pm, Apart from the usual snacks jackets, sandwiches and ploughman's the daily specials like goats cheese crostini and freshly battered cod chips and peas supplement the printed menu. Presently there are seven starters like oven roasted mushrooms with garlic cloves, red onions and tomatoes served on granary toast and half shell green lip mussels grilled with garlic and cream topped with a herb crust. Slow roasted belly of pork with red cabbage and parsnip mash, a slow roasted lamb shank with redcurrant gravy braised vegetable and potatoes and chicken stuffed with Dolcelatte cheese served with crushed parsley potatoes with a pink peppercorn sauce to name but three meat dishes. Vegetarians can choose between baked aubergine stuffed with sun dried tomatoes and garlic cous cous or smoked cheddar and leek tart. Sunday carvery booking advised.

Telephone: 01264 710260 www.theblackswanmonxton.co.uk

Monxton is signed from the A303 at Andover.

You can park in the road at the front or in their own car park 50 yards west along the road.

Approximate distance of walk: 2½ miles. OS map 185. Ref. SU 315/445.

An enjoyable short ramble on field paths, tracks and village streets around Pillhill Brook.

1. Turn right out of the pub or car park and then immediately right at the crossroads and go over the bridge passing the church of St Mary. A short distance, ahead on the bend go up the track on the right leading to Manor Farm. Walk as far as the barn then go left, cross the grass to the stile. When I was here there were llamas in the field on the left. Keep straight ahead all the way out to the road.

2. Turn right then the second turning left walking right up to the end of the cul de sac and bear right. Go up the drive on the left towards the block of four garages then bear right picking up the well walked path. Pass through the kissing gate and continue on the grass path beside the hedge, enter a second field and keep walking to a final gap in the hedge and turn left onto the track which drops gently down to the lane.

3. Turn right, cross Pillhill Brook and continue up the lane until you come to Haydown Links House on the left, footpath is signed. The drive passes between two delightful houses before reaching a grass track leading to a gate. Pass through, turn left and a short way along the track go to the right onto the grass path running beside the fenced horse paddock. Leave by the gap on the far side; follow the path around the lake to the stile then keep to the path ahead which exits at the delightful hamlet of Amport. Bear left across the green and over the plank bridge to the road.

4. Walk straight across into the drive opposite, the green lane marker can be seen on the ground on the right. Walk to the right of the garage block where you will find the fenced path which at one point passes through a kissing gate, for what reason I'm not sure. Join the track, turn left cross both bridges then right into the lane passing the Amport Inn, stop for a quick one if you cannot wait. The route back to the village passes some of the many delightful thatched cottages.

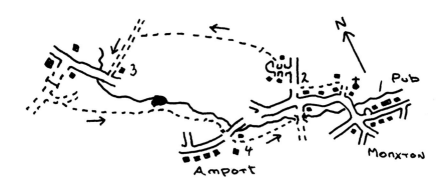

The sketch maps in this book are not necessarily to scale but have been drawn to show maximum amount of detail.

The Red Lion, Oakhanger

You get a friendly welcome in this fine two bar village local converted into a pub from two cottages in 1760. You can take your dog and play darts in the public bar and in the cosy lounge bar/dining room. You can sit by the inglenook fireplace and enjoy the warm log fire in winter.

As Britain slid into recession in the autumn of 2008 the inn started promoting Australian lager not hopefully to the detriment of real ales like Sharps Doom Bar and Ringwood Fortyniner. There is a good wine list.

Food service starts from 12 - 2pm and again from 6.30 - 9pm. There is a printed menu offering a choice of ploughman's, jacket potatoes, burgers, omelettes, sandwiches, baguettes and paninis, soup and a roll etc. If the ham used in the ham ploughman's is an indicator the quality is well above average, The main menu is all on blackboards and seems to have something for all tastes. Choose from 10 oz rib eye steak, gammon steak, pork stroganoff, lasagne, pan fried calves liver, king prawns in garlic, potatoes gnocchi with smoked bacon and mushrooms, battered cod, scampi or delicious sweet and sour chicken with stir fried vegetables. There is a separate a la carte menu in the evening.

Children are welcome inside and there is a delightful grassy rear beer garden.

Opening times are 12 - 3pm and 6 - 11pm (closed Sunday evenings).

Telephone: 01420 472232

Oakhanger can be reached by taking the A325 Borden road south of Farnham, turn right on the B3004 at Sleaford and turn south at Kingsley for 1 mile. The inn is on the main road through the village.

There are car parks front and rear.

Approximate distance of walk: 3¾ miles. OS map 144 Ref. SU 769/359.

A walk on arable farmland and through woods with fine views in places. It has common points with the walks from East Worldham and Selborne and could be used to link or extend these walks. The route selected spends more time than usual on quiet metalled lanes to avoid muddy sections.

1. Turn right out of the pub and cross to the pavement. Pass Lion's Field and reach the attractive thatched cottages on the right. Just past the second cottage "Tunford" turn right over a stile. Keep to the right down the field and cross two stiles at the bottom. Turn left along the field edge and cross a stile at the bottom to a kissing gate. Maintain direction through two more close spaced kissing gates, cross the Oakhanger Stream and go through a gap to a fingerpost. Turn right here following the stream for half a mile until you reach a bridge where cross over and continue, now with the stream on your left.
2. Reach a stile with Priory Farm, site of the former Selborne Priory, down to your left. This point is common to the Selborne walk. Turn right up the track into woods. At a fork go left and cross a stile by a gate. Head slowly right up the field to join a track at the top and continue to bear right uphill with a bank on

your left. Reach two gates and take the right-hand bridleway, a sunken path uphill passing Wick Farm on your left. Continue on a narrow lane to a junction with a bridleway that goes left and two footpaths. The footpath to the right has a notice warning that it is steep and slippery. On our visit it was wet so we avoided it as follows.
3. Turn sharp right on the lane, and at a junction turn right, signed Oakhanger 1 mile. Continue downhill and take the first turning right at a fingerpost signed Hanger Way. This is Candovers. Just past "Candover Barn" turn left off the Hangers Way through a small wooden gate onto a grass path. Leave by a similar gate and go down to a wide crossing track, where turn left down to a road. Turn right down the lane for ¾ of a mile passing the Royal Aerospace Establishment, Telemetry Command Station, on your right and back down to the pub.

OAKHANGER

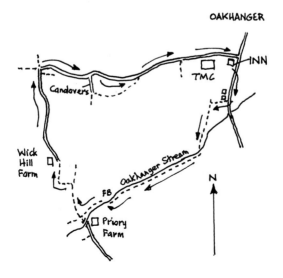

The Water Witch, Odiham

Flower filled tubs and baskets add to the charm of the very pretty Water Witch, parts of which are over 500 years old and housed a well. Similarly the interior is most attractive with old beams festooned with hop vines, two log fires and seating areas divided into booths by panelling. Having closed for a while the pub re-emerged in 2007 as a Chef and Brewers house. There is a very large garden but dining outdoors is restricted to the paved terrace.

As may be expected they have an excellent wine list and the ales are Bombardier, Hog Back T.E.A and a guest, Adnam's Bitter on our visit.

Food is served all day every day. There are extensive snack and main course menus and a blackboard full of daily specials. Among the snacks are a variety of baguettes and toasted baguettes, sandwiches and jacket potatoes and there is a range of small portions - pub standards at reasonable prices e.g. sausages and mash, fish and chips, gammon steak and 6 oz rump steak burgers. Main courses include authentic king prawns, Thai curry, Whitby scampi, sea bass fillet, beef and Bombardier ale pie, pork loin steak, tagliatelle with asparagus and tomato sauce and a mackerel salad. Specials include the like of salmon and monkfish kebab, chicken parmagiano, Moroccan lamb stew and butternut squash and artichoke risotto.

Children are welcome, dogs in the garden only.

Opening times 12 - 10.30pm daily.

Telephone: 01256 702778

Odiham can be reached via the A287 either from junction 5 off the M3 or from Farnham. The pub is in London Road just south of Colt Hill Bridge over the Basingstoke Canal and is signed from the High Street. There is a large car park at the pub.

Approximate distance of walk: 3½ miles. OS map 144. Ref. SU 746/515.

A pleasant walk starting along the Basingstoke Canal towpath and then through North Warnborough and Odiham, where there is much of historical interest. If it is a hot day you might like to know that you pass four more pubs en route and two sites of former pubs - this used to be hop growing country.

1. Turn left out of the pub passing the site of The Cricketers Pub on your left and cross Colt Hill Bridge over the canal. Odiham Wharf is to your right and boat trips and boat hire are available here, but for the walk turn left down the towpath. Pass the simple Lodge Copse Bridge and later go under Swan Bridge, named for The Swan freehouse on the road above that pre-dates the canal. The next bridge is the North Warnborough Swing or Life Bridge. If you want to visit Odiham Castle ruin (see Walk 14) continue along the towpath for about 350 yards and return.

2. Cross the bridge and walk along Tunnel Lane to a T-junction and you are in North Warnborough. Turn right and opposite The Anchor pub turn left on an unsigned gravel drive that soon becomes a footpath. Cross a road and later join a lane passing a school on your left. At a T-junction cross a road and turn left and at Recreation Road turn right and in 40 yards left on a signed footpath.

Continue between fences and cross a road by The Crown pub and soon reach the parish church of All Saints, Odiham. It is usually open and the stained glass windows should not be missed. You are asked not to leave the church without saying a prayer for yourself, your family and friends and the ministers. Stocks and a whipping post outside indicate the fate of those who transgress hereabouts so it might be prudent to kneel and pray! There is a useful information board in front of the church that details all the local buildings of architectural interest in this most attractive old town that repays a wander along the High Street.

3. From the church go forward to The Bell pub, turn left then right to reach the High Street, where cross over and turn right past The George Hotel. Where the road forks keep left on London Road passing the site of the old Angel Inn and back to the pub.

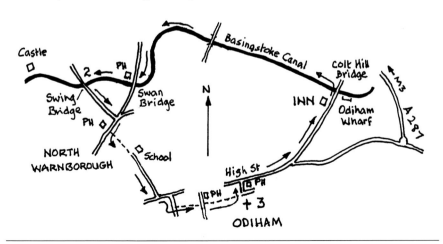

The sketch maps in this book are not necessarily to scale but have been drawn to show maximum amount of detail.

The Queen's College Inn, Pamber End

The Queen's College Inn is a main road Hall & Woodhouse pub which implies certain standards. For a start you are assured of a friendly welcome. The dining areas are situated all around the central bar, pew seats and log burning stoves add a touch of character and there is a nice painting of the Benedictine Priory you passed on the walk.

The selection of real ales may be any three from Badger, Tanglefoot, Sussex, Fursty Ferret, Hopping Hare or Stinger so you really can't go wrong.

As regards the food they leave little to chance as the brewery issues priced menus to the pubs. No doubt there are economies of scale in purchasing and distribution and customers know what to expect. For main courses see the review of The Seven Stars, Stroud (Walk No. 29) Now for the puddings: hand cut chunky fruit salad should supply one of your 'Five a Day' if you pass on the clotted cream ice cream that comes with it. Incidentally in August 2008 there was a basket of apples on the bar with an invitation to 'Take one of your five a day'. Nice one! Eton Mess, chocolate pudding, 'proper' toffee pudding, individual Banoffee pie, berry and almond tart and hot chocolate fudge sundae completes the list all available with Purbeck ice cream made with milk and cream from an Isle of Purbeck 60 strong Friesian herd. In my experience as a walker aggressive/inquisitive Friesians can be a pest so it is nice to see someone putting them to good use. Assorted hot drinks are available for winter walkers.

It is probably worth repeating that children are welcome and starters and main courses are available in half portions to wean them off nuggets and fish shapes. There is also a small assault course in the large garden. Dogs are welcome here but only guide dogs in the pub.

Opening hours are 11.30am - 11pm, Sun 10.30pm and food is served all day from 12 - 9.30pm, Sun 9pm.

Telephone: 01256 850071

The Queens College Inn is situated at Pamber End on the A340, 3 miles north of the junction with the A339 Basingstoke ring road and 1½ miles south of Tadley.

There is a large car park at the front of the pub.

Approximate distance of walk: 4¾ miles. OS map 144. Ref. SU 612/583.

A most enjoyable walk mostly on field paths and woodland bridleways. Part of the route takes you through Pamber Forest Nature Reserve then to the ancient church, returning along a sometimes muddy, overgrown bridleway but improves dramatically through the grounds of the idyllic, moated Wyeford Farm. Finally you visit a 12th century Benedictine Priory church.

1. Leave the pub turning left, cross the road and turn right into Bramley Road. Safely keeping to the right-hand side walk for about a ¼ mile to reach a sign-posted footpath by a gate on the left. Climb the stile into the field, keep to the left and walk to a field opening with woods to the right. Turn right for 25 yards to a stile and footbridge leading into a shaded copse. The path meanders through the trees and boardwalks keep you above the worst of the mud until you reach a road. Cross to the stile opposite and keep ahead beside the fence on the right climbing a couple more stiles to cross two paddocks and on to a third stile that leads out into a field. Turn left for 40 yards to a waymark post then turn right on a narrow path across the centre of a large field. At a fork in the middle of the field keep right to reach the gate to Pamber Forest Nature Reserve.

2. This ancient wood covers an area of 478 acres and is a surviving remnant of the once extensive Royal Forest of Windsor. Keep to the well walked path ahead passing new areas of coppice created as wild life habitats. Go over a crossing path and across a small stream. You should see deer in an enclosure on the left. Keep walking up the slightly

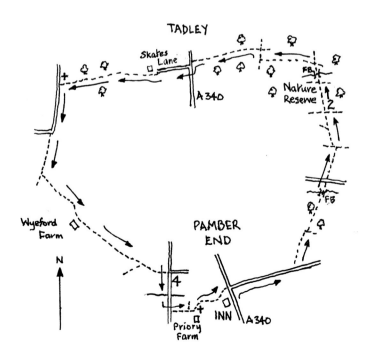

rising track to a crossing path where turn left. Deeply shaded in summer the path meanders between oak trees before reaching a 'T' junction. Turn right, then left at the next crossing path and continue along this attractive route, bearing right at the track junction ultimately reaching the main A340.

3. Turn left, carefully cross over and turn right into Skates Lane. Walk to the end and take the track to the left of the gate to reach another waymarked gate and stile into a field. Keep beside the hedge on the left to a stile in the far corner, then maintaining direction follow a faint path across a field to a stile into woodland. The path leads you through the wood and along a field edge and out into Church Lane just south of St Peter's Church. Sadly as a result of vandalism this simple ancient church is padlocked with wire mesh over the windows. Turn left, ignore a fingerpost on the left and at a sharp corner go ahead on a bridleway (sign post missing in 2008). Mud and nettles may be hazards at first but persevere to find your path lined with bluebells in season and a good chance of

seeing deer. Reach a fork and go through the wide gate on the left and through more attractive woodland until the bridleway veers to the right passing through idyllic moated Wyeford Farm. Slow down and take it all in and note the enormous koi carp in the moat. Continue down the long drive and out to a road.

4. Turn right signed Charter Alley and Ramsden, cross a bridge over a stream and in 150 yards turn left into the gates of Priory Farm. The 12th century church and Benedictine Priory is ahead of you. Walk up to the white farm gate and turn left in front of it and through a wooden gate into the churchyard. The fingerpost was broken in 2008, so turn right to a seat and with your back to the seat bear slightly right between gravestones. Keeping to the left of the two massive oak trees and out into a field, where turn right on a faint grass path. Bear left through a woodland strip over a foot bridge and into a field. Follow the obvious path across the field to a gap in the hedge and out to the A340 and turn right back to the pub.

Pennington, The Musketeer

A warm homely feel pervades throughout this great village local set in the middle of Pennington, a road back from the main village street. Solidly built it has red brick walls under a tilled roof. There is a small seated area close to the side entrance and a larger sunny bar mostly with intimate pew seating and bar stools. Partly wood panelled the room is heated by a warm winter log fire. There is also a separate games/family room. Outside there are wooden benches positioned to make the most of the sunshine

The inn is a freehouse extremely well run by the longstanding licensees who recently celebrated their 25th anniversary at the pub. A good range of drinks is on offer plus a constantly changing selection of well kept real ales which include the likes of Ringwood Best and Fortyniner, Timothy Taylor Landlord and Spitfire from Shepherd and Neame.

The Musketeer is one of a few only non restaurant pubs in the area although food is available 12 - 2pm and 6 - 8pm, Sunday 12 - 4pm. No food Tuesday evenings. The home made selection, is of excellent quality and includes the usual pub fayre.

Live music Friday, Saturday and Sunday night, quiz night Tuesday.

Children and dogs welcome, but there is a separate room for small children.

Opening times: Monday - Thursday 11.30 - 2.30pm and 5 - 11.30pm. Friday and Saturday all day 11.30 - 12.00am. Sunday all day 12 - 11pm.

Telephone: 01590 676527

Walk No. 25

From Brockenhurst take the A337 to Lymington following it to the first roundabout and turn right into North Street.

Rear car park at the pub, public parking opposite plus limited parking in the lane at the front.

Approximate distance of walk: 5¼ miles. OS map Outdoor Leisure 22. Ref. 950/311.

An interesting and enjoyable walk exploring the footpaths, lanes and by-ways around Pennington. Although mostly flat some areas can be very wet in the winter.

1.Turning right from the pub then right again continue along the approach road, past the church, turning right once more in the road leading to the recreation ground (signposted). Continue along the lane (footpath sign-posted) and just before reaching the house at the end climb the stile on the right, turning right along the grass path to reach the metal gate. Follow the hedge line ahead which bears right then left before reaching a small bridge. On the far side climb the stile into the field and bear left to a second stile then simply follow the narrow, twisting path up to the Sway road.

2. Go straight across to the track opposite, and beyond the dwellings join the narrow bluebell lined path on the left leading to a stile then drops down the bank, passes a dwelling and enters a field. Walk to the far corner, turn right, and at the finger post turn left walking up between the dwellings and across the drive to the stile. Follow the path ahead, up to the lane and turn left.

3. At the road, bearing right, cross over into Mill Lane. The prominent tower at Arnewood Court can be clearly seen in the distance. Turn left into the lane, past a couple of fine dwellings then turn right into Flexford Lane.

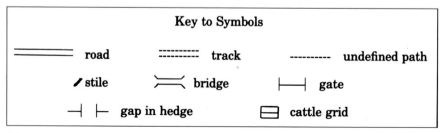

Key to Symbols

road	track	undefined path
stile	bridge	gate
gap in hedge		cattle grid

Cross the bridge and turn left onto the track (footpath signposted). In a short distance bear left past the stable block to the stile at the end. The grass area ahead leads to a concealed stile in the right-hand corner. Keep to the narrow wire-fenced path, up to a second stile then up to the road.

4. Briskly cross to the track opposite following it all the way ahead, through a couple of gates into Batchley Farm yard. Occasional patches of wild daffodils and primroses brighten the route. Bear right, and in a few paces take the sign-posted footpath on the left beside the tractor shed. Cross the stile into the field, past the bluebell wood to the bottom and take the path on the left, crossing the drive to Wainsford Farm and up to the road turning left.

5. Keep to the right-hand side, cross the bridge and a short distance up the hill just by the "road narrows" sign join the signed footpath on the right, which meanders its way through a small copse, the route marked with occasional yellow topped posts. Turn right into the road and continue ahead back to the village walking, if you prefer, on the edge of the common. Just before reaching the main road fork right straight back to the pub.

The Shoe Inn, Plaitford

On a trip to the Forest The Shoe is a must. Built in 1420 a beautifully crafted thatched roof protects the original inn, which took its name from the cavalry troops who frequented the inn when travelling from the garrison in Salisbury to the port of Marchwood. Seen from the main road, it's an attractive, black and white half timbered structure, which was a posting station for mail coaches. A tollgate was constructed across the road and the landlord made responsible for collecting the King's tolls. The interior of the Shoe is as inviting as the outside having old world charm, real fires and many bygones on display.

The New Forest highwayman, John Taylor was caught drinking here and subsequently hanged on nearby Plaitford Common. Queen Victoria once stopped here on route to the Isle of Wight. Along side the inn is what used to be the main road between Salisbury and Southampton.

The Shoe is a freehouse well run by the hosts Jeni and Aart Noordijk offering a good selection of lagers, draught beers, and extensive choice of wines plus three real ales.

Food is available every lunchtime and evening. On offer is an appetising choice of home-made soups and starters, various main dishes, daily specials like shank of lamb and T bone steaks and some irresistible *'go on indulge yourself'* home-made sweets. In good weather you can enjoy your meal in the attractive garden.

Well behaved dogs are welcome in the bar together with children.

Entertainment includes pool, darts, dominoes, Irish & folk music on Friday evenings and Blues and Rock on Sunday evening.

Opening times 11 - 3ish and 6 - 11pm, Sunday 12 - 3pm and 6 - 10pm.

Accommodation: Five charming bedrooms.

Telephone: 01794 322397. email: theshoeinn@btinternet.com

Pub located on the A36 on the Hampshire/Wiltshire border between Southampton and Salisbury.

Car park beside the pub and on the opposite side of the road. Alternatively you can park in Sherfield English Road, a few steps away.

Approximate distance of walk: 4¼ miles. OS map Landranger 183. Ref. 276/194.

A very enjoyable walk especially if you walk in late spring and want to see bluebells. The first section is mostly on field and woodland paths, the last mile and a half is on peaceful country lanes. It is an easy going mostly level walk but can be a bit wet in winter and early spring.

1. Leave the pub turning right and, almost immediately, turn right into Sherfield English Road. Walk for a short distance until you reach the sign-posted footpath on the left, go a short distance up the drive then bear right and join the raised narrow track. Generally good underfoot it is lined with primroses with areas of periwinkle and arum lilies. When the path reaches a field continue ahead close to the hedge on the right then go to the right of the house, out into the lane and turn right.

2. Walk for a while reaching the track on the left (footpath sign-posted) a short way ahead bear right by a finger-post, across an area of grass guided by yellow dots on trees leading to a bridge. Snowdrops can be seen close to the river bank early in the year. Beyond the bridge continue following the marked path, up into and through the bluebell wood eventually reaching a stile. Bearing right go up the field (can be wet here in winter) through the removal wire fence, to the right of the dwelling and onto the track.

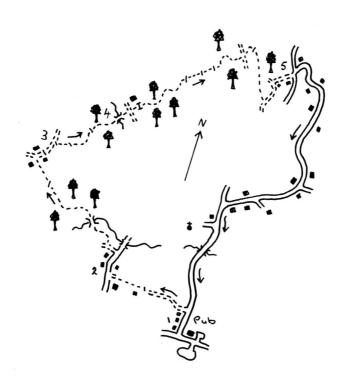

3. Turn right through the gate and, after walking along the track just a few paces climb the stile into the field on the right. Cross to the opposite stile, through the small bluebell wood, up to stile and climb into the field then turn immediately right. Walk to the bottom, through another section of woodland and up to the bridge.

4. Cross the river back into Hampshire and keep straight ahead, over the track, through the kissing gate following the path ahead up through the trees, the route marked once more by yellow spots on trees and posts. Upon reaching the stile cross the field to the stile just visible in the far boundary beyond which maintain direction across the field and enter the bluebell wood. Keep to the main path through this glorious wood which eventually meets a track at which point turn left then bear right up to the road at Plaitford Green

5. Cross over into Flowers Lane the hedgerows of which are dotted with the occasional clump of wild daffodils and patches of snowdrops. Bear right at the junction staying on the lane back to the main road turning left back to the pub.

The Selborne Arms, Selborne

Entering the handsome 17th Century Selborne Arms free house past a board boasting that it had been chosen as the Hampshire Life Dining Pub of the Year 2008, we had visions of a ghastly gastropub offering fine dining and wining but no real ale. Not so, two charming barmaids pointed to an array the like of which is seldom seen. I scribbled furiously fearful that this was a mirage and would evaporate - Ringwood's Fortyniner, Arundel Gold, King's Summer Ale, Palmer's Copper Ale, Bloomfield's Bitter, Bowman's Swift One, then enter a drayman with a cask of Goddard's Fuggle Bee Bum. A regular said "I don't know why you are writing them down they will all be changed next week!" Wonderful, every village should have a Selborne Arms.

The pub looks its age with exposed beams and log fires. There are separate rooms at both ends of a long bar. Outside is a raised and covered patio, which makes an unusually luxurious smokers' retreat, and a pleasant garden where one table has two chessboards set into the surface.

A printed bar menu offers ploughman's lunches in local ham or a choice of six cheeses individually or mixed to your choice. There are baguettes and jacket potatoes, plaice goujons, salmon and broccoli fishcakes and the like. Children are catered for with things children apparently like but also with small portions of dishes that they may learn to like, including Sunday roasts. The blackboard menus are extensive and excellent and cooked well enough to win awards. I just couldn't read it without my glasses.

Dogs are welcome in the garden only, where water bowls are supplied.

Opening hours are Monday-Saturday 11-3pm and 6-11pm and Sunday 12-10.30pm.

Food service is from 12-2pm and 7-9pm.

Telephone: 01420 51147

Walk No. 27

Selborne is on the B3006 and can be reached by turning south off the A31 at Alton or north off the A3 at Greatham for approximately 3½ miles.

The inn is on the B3006 in front of the National Trust car park that also serves as the pub car park.

Approximate distance of the walk: 3½ miles. OS map 133. Ref. SU 742/335.

Selborne was the home of the eminent 18th century naturalist Gilbert White, whose observations of the local flora and fauna over a 40 year period were published in 1789. This walk visits some of his favourite places, his house "Wakes" which is open to the public, and the 12th century St Mary's Church, where there is a commemorative stained glass window depicting St Francis of Assisi preaching to the 82 birds mentioned in White's book. The first part of the walk uphill can be hard going and an option to omit the climb is given. There may be mud in the woods in sections 2 and 3.

1. Turn right out of the pub and right again to the car park. Take the path to the left of the car park entrance signed 'Zig Zag Path and Hangers' and go uphill to a kissing gate. If you do not fancy the climb take the lower path to the right, called 'Love Lane' by the locals, cross a stile on the right and cross a meadow to another stile and maintain direction down a lane to the B3006. "Wakes" is just along on the right. Otherwise, bear left from the kissing gate up the Zig Zag path cut by White and his brother John in 1753. At the top go right on the stepped path and in a few yards fork right through the beech hangers. A bench affords a fine view of the church and "Wakes". Continue downhill to a junction of paths by a National Trust sign. Turn right downhill on a track and where

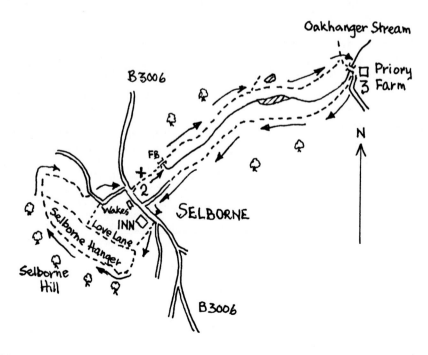

this goes left look out for a stile on the right into a field. Keep to the left hand edge of the field over three more stiles and out to a lane, where turn right to reach the B3006. "Wakes" is just along on the right.

2. From "Wakes" cross the road diagonally left to a small car park and follow a fingerpost signed 'Hangers Way and Alton' into the churchyard. You pass the remains of a 1400 years old Yew tree blown down in 1990 and White's grave is signed to the rear. Continue through the churchyard and out through a kissing gate, then down to a footbridge over the Oakhanger Stream signed Hangers Way. Negotiate two more kissing gates and there are now nice views down into the valley bottom. The stream is concealed by trees but the slopes are covered in wild flowers. After the next kissing gate the path forks and you leave the Hangers Way to follow the yellow arrow right, soon between two attractive small lakes with much wildlife. Cross a stile and go through woods to another stile and then along the left hand side of a long field to a stile that leads out to a fenced bridleway. Turn right, cross the stream and enter a farmyard. This is Priory Farm on the site of the former Selborne Priory.

3. Keep to the right through the farmyard and outside bear right past a fingerpost on a track passing a house on your left. Go through a gate and keep to the left hand side of the fields through two more gates then into woods. This path is known as the Monks' Walk from the Priory to the village. Pass a house 'Dorton's' and go up hill to join Huckers Lane which leads back to the village. At the B3006 turn left back to the pub.

Remains of 1400 years old yew tree, St Mary's Church Selborne

St Francis preaching to the birds, St Mary's Church Selborne

81

Hatchet Inn, Sherfield English

This family friendly pub has recently come under new management and nicely refurbished but still managing to retain many of the original features including the oak beams. There is seating at the front outside and a child and toddlers area next to the car park.

The well stocked bar includes four real ales Ringwood Best, Adnams, Abbot Ale plus a rotating guest ale and wines from around the globe.

Food is served every day 12 - 2pm and 5 - 9pm and has distinctly eastern flavour. Beside the usual lunchtime bar snack which include a delicious choice of baguettes and jackets, bar snacks like home-made steak and kidney pie, locally made sausages with bubble and squeak ham, egg and chips plus pan fried liver and bacon, the main menu will usually include a selection of starters for all tastes like sizzling duck with mixed vegetables in hoi sin sauce, home-made crab cakes with a sweet chilli dip, crayfish tails on a bed of rocket with lime dressing, deep fried breaded vegetable dip, pan fried prawns with garlic and parsley and deep fried brie with rhubarb. For fish lovers there is sole fillets stuffed with crab and scallops on a cucumber sauce, fillet of sea bass on Singapore noodles, Main courses could range from slow roasted lamb shank on sweet potato mash with mint gravy, half a roast duck with prune and apple sauce, half a roast pheasant on braised red cabbage and Port jus, guinea fowl supreme with a winter berry sauce and sizzling chicken fajitas. All tastes are catered for from the exotic Bison steak with a Port and Stilton sauce, pasta such as wild mushroom ravioli and a vegetarian roasted red onion and cheese tart. There is a special menu for children including half portions of most dishes. Monday to Friday there is a 'kids eat free offer.' from 5.30 - 7pm. Thursday night is a two for one steak night. Children very welcome and dogs too on a lead but not in dining room when food is being served. Opening times Monday to Thursday 12 - 3pm and 6 - 11pm, Friday, Saturday and Sunday all day 12 - 11pm.

Telephone: 01794 322487 www. hatchetinn.com

Village signed from the A27 east of Romsey.

There is a good front car park plus limited space at the side in Mill Lane.

Approximate distance of walk: 4 miles. OS map Landranger 184/185. Ref. 292/224.

A delightful mostly level easy going walk on field and woodland paths, tracks and peaceful country lanes. It is ideal for all members of the family.

1. Leave the pub carefully crossing over into the track opposite. Walk for a while until you reach a waymark post on the right, it is marked with a yellow disc, at this point enter the field on the left and make your way up to the stile in the far top right-hand corner. Continue along the hedge line following it round and out through the gate then continue ahead through a gate at the corner of the wood and head straight down the field to the stile, climb over out to the lane and turn left.

2. Go past the dwellings turning right onto the track at the end of Church Lane. Keep straight ahead at the cross rack, past the dwellings walking until you reach a lane then turn left and walk to the main road.

3. Carefully cross over to the unmade road opposite following it round to the left, past all the dwellings and up to the T junction at which point turn right. Walk past the large lily pond taking time to look out for dragonflies and other insects then take the left fork keeping straight ahead on this gavel road that rises steadily passing Melchet Park Farm. When you see the finger post on the left join the narrow path which skirts round the edge of the grand looking house before

reaching a gate and track beyond.

4. Upon reaching the stile, climb into the field and, staying close to the hedge, walk to the stile on the far side and cross over into the bluebell wood. Marked with the occasional yellow dot the path winds through a mix of deciduous woodland. After crossing a track look for a small wooden finger post at which point turn left. You will see small yellow arrows painted on the trees. The path leads to a small plank bridge and garden gate, goes into a field and re-enters the wood. After leaving by another gate the path continues straight ahead through the trees to reach another gate leading into a field then follows the hedge boundary ahead finally passing through one last garden gate before reaching the lane.

5. Bearing left cross to the stile and sign-posted footpath opposite, over another crossing point and into the field. Keeping to the boundary walk almost to the end of the field then bear right in the direction of the dwelling, cross to the hedge gap and turn left into the lane. After passing some very attractive cottages, turn left at the T junction following the peaceful lane back to the pub.

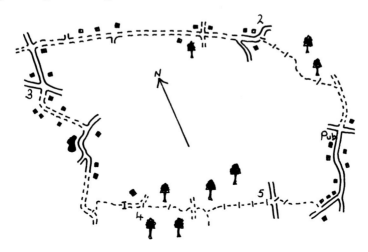

The Seven Stars, Stroud

The 18th century brick and flint built Seven Stars is set back from the A272 and shielded from the road by a weeping willow and a duck pond resplendent at times with irises and bulrushes. Bench seating is arranged on the grass round the pond and in front of the pub and the whole thing makes an enticing sight for passers-by. The interior is spacious, running in front of and both ends of a long bar with log fires and a log burning stove spaced at intervals. At one end a barn conversion has been incorporated as a dining extension and features original beams and an interesting pew seat with built-in storage.

Hall and Woodhouse owned, the ales are Badger, Tanglefoot and Fursty Ferret with seasonal variations and there is an excellent list of reasonably priced wines.

The standard menu prepared by the brewery rather than pub management is extensive and it is hard to think of anything not represented here. There is a good choice of sandwiches, baguettes and jackets and a soup of the day. Salads are goat's cheese, chicken Caesar and grilled salmon. Pub standards include fish and chips, scampi, ham and eggs and gourmet burger. Vegetarians are catered for with roast vegetable tart and summer vegetable pie. Several featured dishes include steak and Tanglefoot pie, and the 'Famous Sussex Smokey' of white and smoked fish, tomato and spinach in cheese sauce topped with savoury crumble. A specials board offered tuna steak topped with pesto and roasted vegetables and butternut squash filled with courgettes, mushrooms and pine nuts. Children are encouraged to try a half portion of anything on the starter and main course menu.

Children are welcome and there is a slide in the garden. Dogs are welcome on the left hand side of the bar.

Opening times are 11am-11pm daily and food is served all day from 12 - 9pm, Sunday 12 - 8.30pm.

Telephone: 01730 231362

Stroud is on the A272 Winchester to Petersfield road ¾ mile west of the junction with the A3 at Petersfield. The pub is set back on the south side of the road and has a large car park.

Approximate distance of walk 2½ miles. OS map 133. Ref. SU 723/236.

A scenic walk on farm tracks, field and woodland paths, particularly notable for bluebells in season and wildlife. Sightings of deer are common and game birds everywhere. There are a couple of short steep sections aided by earth steps but no handrails that could be a bit tricky when wet.

1. Leave the pub turning left and immediately go left again into Ramsdean Road. Just beyond Languish Primary School take the signposted footpath on the right through a kissing gate into a field. Bear half right to a squeeze stile in a fence, then through a kissing gate and straight ahead to the kissing gate opposite, finally bearing left across the grass and out to a lane. Cross to the signposted footpath opposite and negotiate the plank bridge and stile into a field. Keep straight ahead over a couple more stiles then maintain direction up a grassy hill to a stile into woodland. Follow the bluebell fringed path up through the wood and into the field at the top. Turn right along the field edge to a corner, where bear left as directed by a finger post across the field to a stile in the far hedge. Walk down then up the field to a stile, then immediately turn right on a farm track for about 500 yards to reach the A272.

2. Turn right, cross over and just past the white house turn left on the signposted footpath. Head straight up the field past the central power pole to a stile into woods. Look back for the view then go up steep steps to a fingerpost and across the field as directed. You may have to shimmy your way through

head high maize here as we found the path planted over. Head for a farm track through a field opening, go down a slope and follow the track right. Keep to the right and soon join a grass footpath running parallel to and above the track. There were snipe, a kestrel and literally dozens of red legged partridge and pheasant along here. Keep ahead at a fingerpost and the path rejoins the earlier track before it enters woodland. This is Great Hanger.

3. Do not enter the woodland. There is a partly concealed yellow waymark arrow on a fence post on the right and you turn right here beside the boundary. In 100 yards take the signed left turn to join a track going downhill. Keep left and at a fork go left to a stile by a gate and into a field. Bear half left to a stile in the far corner then, maintaining direction, cross to a stile into a woodland strip. Go carefully down steep steps into a field and over the field to a stile. Turn right on a grass path and at a fingerpost on the right cross a stile into a field and in a few yards bear half left to a stile in the far corner. Follow the hedge line to one last stile, finally turning right onto the farm track leading back to the pub.

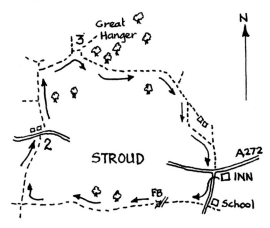

The Barley Mow, Winchfield Hurst

From the front the big square Barley Mow dominating the crossroads looks plain and in need of a few more tubs and baskets of flowers to soften its appearance. After a period of closure it was refurbished and re-opened in 2007 and probably needs a little time to mellow again. The village green and cricket pitch are behind the pub and it certainly comes of life when the team is playing. Inside an L-shaped bar services the long room at the front and another at the side that leads to a conservatory. Armchairs and leather settees make this a very comfortable interior in which to sample the ales - Old Hookey, Black Sheep, London Pride and Ruddles Country and to chat to the welcoming and helpful bar staff.

  Food service is Monday - Friday 12 - 3pm and 6.30 - 9.30pm, Saturday 12 - 2.30pm and 6 - 9.30pm, Sunday 12 - 5pm. There are separate standard lunch and dinner menus. Snacks include baguettes, ciabattas or wraps with a choice of eight fillings including brie, bacon and cranberry and beef, horseradish and watercress. Jacket potato fillings include curry of the day and smoked salmon with cream cheese. The chicken Caesar salad was the best we have seen proving that the addition of tomatoes makes all the difference to the appearance and the taste. Home-made soup comes in two bowl sizes with crusty bread. Beer battered fresh fish of the day, grilled sardines, penne pasta and green vegetables in a white wine sauce, sausage of the day with spring onion mash indicate imaginative variety that must make the chef's job more interesting as well as pleasing the customers, particularly when taking into account the specials board that changes daily. Offerings may include mahi mahi, salmon steak and tiger prawns, seared swordfish on cous cous, various steaks, calves liver and bacon and spiced duck breast with beetroot cassis and rosemary cream. There is a choice of three roasts on Sundays.

  Children and dogs are welcome inside and out with the proviso that the dogs do not set foot on the carpets, effectively the dining areas.

  Opening hours are Monday - Friday 12 - 3pm and 5.30 - 11.30pm Saturday 12 - 11.30pm and Sunday 12 - 10.30pm.

  Telephone: 01252 617490

From Junction 5 on the M3 turn south on the A287. After 1.5 miles turn left on the B3016, then take the first right, Bagwell Lane. At a T-junction turn right and at a cross roads turn right into Winchfield Hurst. The Barley Mow is on the left at the next crossroad.

There is ample parking at the pub.

Approximate distance of walk: 5¼ miles. OS map 186. Ref. SU 778/539.

This walk is courtesy of Sir Henry Mildmay who owned Dogmersfield Park in the late 18th/early 19th centuries. He refused the Basingstoke Canal Company permission to take the canal across his land, so forcing a detour to the north and adding over a mile to the canal's length. The walk takes in over 3 miles of towpath and in between crosses the parkland, visiting picturesque Tundry Pond and with a section through woodland that may be muddy in winter.

1. From the front of the pub cross the road and go up Sprat's Hatch Lane and in a few yards turn left through the pub's overflow car park to the canal towpath and turn left. After one mile along this pleasant stretch turn right over Blacksmith's Bridge. Cross a stile and turn right then left on a path to reach the shore of Tundry Pond which presents an attractive pastoral scene with cattle and sheep grazing, swans and other birds on the water and two bridges at the far end. Head towards the three arched bridge, then turn left through a kissing gate and up a gravel drive. Dogmersfield House is ahead of you.

2. At a cattle grid take the first signed footpath on your right then maintain direction on a surfaced road. Pass two houses on your right and go ahead uphill at first on a track. Where power lines pass overhead fork right through a kissing gate onto a fenced path. You get a nice glimpse of Dogmersfield Lake on your right before joining a gravel drive between two lodge houses, then turn right at a fingerpost on a path into woodland. This wood does not appear to be managed as fallen trees littering the path made our progress interesting. Ignore a waymarked path to the left and reach a green painted metal gate where turn

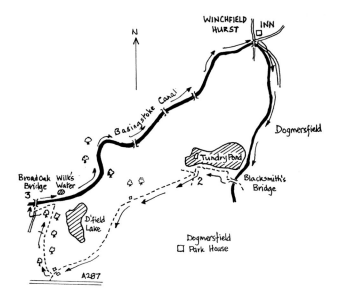

left (the waymark is stuck on a silver birch tree). The narrow path soon joins the canal bank then soon reaches a small car park.

3. Turn right over Broad Oak Bridge and turn right again along the towpath. This is an attractive section of the canal where there may be barges and other boats to add interest. On the left early on is Wilk's Water a very pretty pond framed with weeping willows that is usually home to a family of mute swans. There are five more nicely restored brick bridges to pass under and after Barley Mow Bridge turn up left through the car park and back to the pub.

Tundry Pond

Barley Mow Bridge, Basingstoke Canal